ild we lived on the north side of Cork City, in Ireland.

ous building and landmark in the city is the church of St
on. Also on the hilly north side, a spectacular and wonderful
ing , surveying all of the city below it. With its four clock
be   wn locally as 'the four-faced liar'. Each of the clocks could
loo   ve a different time, depending on which clock you were
their   elieve many a young man and woman were often late for
                hey were depending on Shandon.

Flying m   ically on top of Shandon is a golden fish, from our house I
could he   e bells, see the clocks and wonder at the wonderful fish. In
my sorro   and grief, I too wanted to fly away, so after a period of time
and a fe   tempts at flying, I climbed a high wall behind our house
again an   ter a few practice take offs, I was ready. One, two, three –
running   fast as I could, I attempted my flight. Alas, I fell to the yard
below an   roke my arm.

A lifetim   has passed since those childhood days, gone as fast, as they
say, as a New York heartbeat, broken dreams, broken promises, good
times, ba   times, and ordinary times. The golden fish is still flying
majestica   looking out over Cork City, and I'm still learning to fly.

And I Thought I Could Fly

Tom Cronin

Copyright © 2010 Tom Cronin

The moral right of the author has been asserted.

Matador
5 Weir Road
Kibworth Beauchamp
Leicester LE8 0LQ, UK
Tel: (+44) 116 279 2299
Fax: (+44) 116 279 2277
Email: books@troubador.co.uk
Web: www.troubador.co.uk/matador

ISBN 978 1848763 548

British Library Cataloguing in Publication Data.
A catalogue record for this book is available from the British Library.

Typeset by Troubador Publishing Ltd, Leicester, UK
Printed and bound in Great Britain by TJI Digital, Padstow, Cornwall

Matador is an imprint of Troubador Publishing Ltd

MIX
Paper from
responsible sources
FSC® C013056

This book is dedicated to all those who have been abused as children or adults.

When you purchase this book, you will be helping vulnerable children.

Thank you.

For more information go to www.irishabusesurvivors.com

DIS. A

SEAMAN'S RECORD BOOK ANI

with a Copy
of the MASTER'

Name of Seaman, in full	Date of Birth
Thomas Brendan Cronin	18TH APRIL, 1951

Height		Colour of		Complexion
feet	inches	(1) eyes	(2) hair	
5	9	(1) HAZEL (2) FAIR		FRESH

Irish Seaman's Identity Card No. 2873

DECLARATION

I DECLARE (i) that the person to whom this Discharge Book relates has satisfied me that he is a seaman and (ii) that the photograph affixed bearing my official stamp is a true likeness of that person, that the signature within is his true signature, that he possesses the physical characteristics entered within and has stated to me the date and place of his birth as entered within.

SIGNATURE OF SUPERINTENDENT AT MERCANTILE MARINE OFFICE—

T. O'Riain

Date 16/1/67

PHOTOGRAPH OF HOLDER

CHAPTER ONE

Casablanca and Beyond

September 1967, Cork City Ireland I am sixteen years of age. A tall skinny not very well dressed, hungry, bad toothed, holes in my shoes kid. But I had a good job, one that I had dreamt of for as long as I can remember, deck boy on a ship. The M.V Uskbridge a cargo ship with 5 hatches Cork to Casablanca carrying phosphate for Gouldings, where the fuck was Casablanca? Somewhere in Africa o' the wages around £8.00 a week a kings ransom in that day and age for a sixteen year old. I remember years earlier I had been on a radio programme called the School around the corner, the presenter Paddy Crosby asked me if I had ever been outside of Ireland, yes sir said I "where says he" all ears, up the Mardyke, says I little did I know the truth, that the Mardyke was just a suburb of Cork. Now here I was at last really outside Cork, Ireland and on my way to Casablanca.

Cork City was a depressing place in the 50s early 60s as I remember it, conservative Catholic not much work a lot of emigration husbands who drank too much, spent all their dole money and then beat their wives and their kids of which families of 10 to 18 children was not uncommon living in one or two bedroom tenement houses. However a lot of these "Ghetto" houses had been knocked down, the Marsh being one of these areas and being replaced by new houses in Gurrnabraher and later Churchfield and Spangle hill renamed Farranree on the north side and Ballypheane and Togher on the south side. The river lee being the natural and dividing force between both the north and south with

1

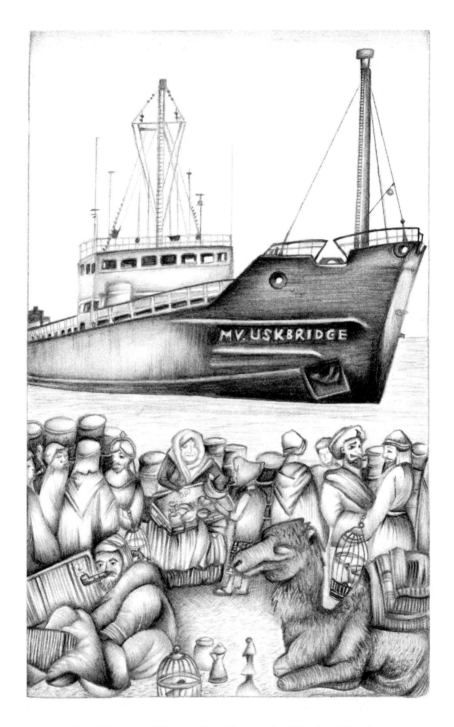

Casablanca… Johnny One Eye… And Dodgy Watches

one north channel running under the North Gate Bridge, Patrick's bridge etc. and the south channel running under the South Gate Bridge before rejoining below the city at Tivoli and carrying on down past Black Rock Lough Manon and Cobh before finally reaching the sea.

Harry Darcy, Dennis Mc Cairn, from Cobh, John Coughlan from Kinsale were all seamen at this time. It took us about 8 days to get to Africa through the Bay of Biscay which I was to learn in the following months could be one of the roughest area's of sea in the world. O God, I was sea sick on the first voyage but that could not stop my sense of adventure and excitement of sailing to Africa. Best of food, cigarettes, my own cabin full of photographs of the most beautiful woman in different stages of undress that I ever had the good fortune to see and getting paid as well, I thought I'd died and gone to heaven.

Casablanca

Can you just imagine coming from Ireland and arriving in a very warm North Africa seeing these strangely dressed looking people speaking in a foreign language, for me, well it was like landing on the moon. Hubblely, Bubbley Pipes, Strange Birds, Jeans and dodgy watches for a £1. The story goes that there was a small cockroach inside of these watches and that when you got past Cape Finister the cockroach died, end of watch.

The ship had now docked and all of the crew were going about their jobs, part of my job was to make sure that the crew get their meals etc. on entering the mess room I overheard one of the seaman in deep negotiations with one of the Arabs, a dodgy looking character by the name of Johnny One Eye. I believe he lost his eye in some fight or other. On listening closer and to my horror, the seaman was selling me, I couldn't believe my ears, but he seemed serious, anyway negotiations broke down, when the Arab was prepared only to offer one pair of jeans and one dirty book. The seaman wanted two dirty books, I certainly learned a good lesson that day, don't ever overvalue your worth. Looking back now and thinking about it there are not that many Irish in the world, I wonder what my worth would have been had I been Chinese. I also know now that there are a lot of Johnny One Eye's in the world and I seem to have met most of them.

The days ran into weeks, weeks into months, and I settled into my life and all seemed very well taking my turn at the wheel, painting, lookout and learning to splice. The first day I was to report to the bridge to take the wheel, the first mate asked me to get the log. I didn't have a clue, what was he talking about, was it a log for the fire or what? After searching around for about 10 minutes I asked one of the seaman, and taking pity on me he showed me what it was, for those of you that don't know it records the distance covered by the ship, so it looks like a little clock with a long string trailing from it, in the water behind the ship. So the work was hard, but I liked the life yes, I decided a seaman's life was for me and especially when we could go ashore, on one occasion in Casablanca a group of us decided to go to the seaman's mission, however on the way we found this dance hall and decided to go in, once inside the drink started to flow, and in a very short time I was, to say the least a little under the weather, the group that were playing were the Rolling Stones, looking back they weren't even related to musician's never mind the Rolling Stones, at the interval they came down to the bar, which we had propped up since we arrived. In my half drunken state I persuaded them that I was a drummer, the best to come out of Ireland, and I could if they asked me nicely, sit in on a few numbers with them.

O la la la le Bamba "Jesus Christ" what was I doing up here, on the stage with these people gathered around thinking they were going to hear the master at work, boy were they disappointed, the band started again A one, two, One two three four, or French words to that effect. O la la la le Bamba, da,da,da,da... but I couldn't hear a thing, so with that the crowd started to Boo, and Boo and began throwing things at the stage and particularly at me, no need to tell you I got off the stage like fast, finishing my drumming career, and never got back on a stage again, O yes I was going to make a much better seaman.

Back and forth, The Mediterranean, the Bay of Biscay, the Atlantic, the South Irish Sea, September turned to October, November, December and talk of Christmas, we would be in Port on Christmas Day everybody hoped we would but unfortunately it was not to be. We sailed from Cork around the 21st of December. On Christmas Eve I was on watch on the foxel head when it struck 12:00 midnight I remember looking over the bow, there were some porpoises racing along and leaving a trail in the water. They looked as if they were playing and having good fun.

It was pitch black and there were no stars in the sky, for the first time in a long time I felt very lonely and sad, but before I had too much time to start thinking about things my relief came and I went to my cabin and had a good nights sleep, those porpoises put me to sleep that night and on many a night since then, when I have been troubled I have gone back to that night and those beautiful porpoises, they have never failed to ease my troubles and make me tranquil again. New Years Day was also spent at sea but that did not have the same effect on me as Christmas Day, the day I made some new friends.

Prostitutes

The Lady's of the night are in every port as every seaman knows, and Cork was no different in those days. I got my first taste of those Lady's very early on, let me explain.

Being the deck boy, I was required to "when in port" to call the Cook in the mornings at 6:30 or 7:00am, so rather than go home and have to rise at say 5am, I decided to go back to the ship late at night and sleep on board, I was installed in my cabin all ready for a nights sleep when someone started banging on my Cabin door, on opening it two young ladies barged in, and told me some other member of the crew had been chasing them, so I allowed them to stay and after a short while one of them decided she wanted to stay, things were starting to look up, anyway we talked but I never made a move on her, she stayed all night and left in the morning after I brought her breakfast. After the weekend the Captain was very upset, it seems the ship took on water on Friday, which would normally last two weeks however with all of the business being done on the ship, the lady's were constantly taking showers and used all of the ships water.

Johnnie One Eye, Hashes and the rest, I got to know all of the Arabs that used to trade with our ship, I remember one particular night we were at anchor in Casablanca waiting to leave, when I was informed that I was to be night watchman, a lot of the crew got a launch and went ashore, so it looked as if I was going to have an easy night, so I done my rounds every hour checked the anchorage, lights etc. so one o'clock turned to two but I felt o.k. not tired the only thing

I had to remember was to call the Cook at 6am. No problem. I'm not sure if you know or not but it gets very cold in North Africa at night being near the desert is I suspect the reason. Around 5am, I felt a little drowsy, could I risk a little sleep before I went to wake the Cook, before I knew it I was fast asleep, someone was shaking me wake up, wake up. Ah, ah what's wrong I said as I began to come round, it was the Cook waking me up, he never reported me for my lapse, but never let me forget it either. Backwards and forwards, Cork to Casablanca rough seas, calm seas, good day's, bad day's Arabs one side, Irish the other side, yes my real education had begun. On my bunk one calming evening somewhere in the Mediterranean I began to reminisce about the years that had brought me to this point in my life. I was looking but not seeing, I was now tranced in my past.

My mother, who died at the tender age of 28 years

The Die is Cast. My Mother has Died

CHAPTER TWO

My Mother's Death – The Die is Cast

My mother died when I was two or three years of age, I remember her dying. She had pneumonia but would not go to hospital as I now believe there was nobody to look after myself and my two older brothers, my father was fond of the drink as was the saying, in fact he was a drunkard, and was involved in gambling also. So I think we were on a highway to nowhere from day one. Just before my mother died, I can remember she had not eaten her tea which consisted of a cake and a cup of tea, she gave me the cake it was a biscuit cake, so biscuit cakes will always bring back that memory to me, strange this. The first car, I ever rode in was the funeral car and all to soon, my mother by the way was only 28 years, was gone, and soon forgotten. After this our father used to lock us in our bedroom at about 6 o'clock in the evening and go to the Dog track, where I believe he worked as a bookies clerk. One game myself, and my brothers, played when we were locked in our bedroom was to look out of the window and if a man passed it would be one point for one, and if a woman passed it would be one point for the other. I don't remember whoever won this game but I'm sure it must have passed some time for us. Around this time also I got it into my head that I could fly. So I went to the shed of the back of the house and gave a run off the shed which was probably about 12 foot high, flapped my hands and arms and, for my trouble, broke my arm.

Through neglect, I developed pneumonia myself, and was

hospitalised for what seemed like a long time. There was another boy in the bed next to mine and he was allowed home the day before me, as he was leaving he cleared his locker and gave me the biggest bag of biscuits ever, they were called Town Ice I believe. You know the type with different letters on them, I dreamt about them all night long. However when they told me I could go home in my haste to get out I forgot and left them in my locker. Little did I know what I was rushing out to.

Ireland in the Fifties

Ireland in the fifties was not a very pleasant place to grow up in especially for the working class, there was still mass emigration mostly to England and poverty was rife. Where we lived which was St. Anthony's Road Gurranbraher on the Northside of the City the neighbours were everything, and I know that our next door neighbours were more than good to us with food etc. It so sad to note that today we still have mass emigration from our country the only difference now is that most of the emigrants are well educated where in the past this was not the case. Successive Governments and the Bureaucrats should hold their heads in shame. It seems the more things change the more they stay the same but then I have often thought that there must be some form of hidden agenda.

You would have to credit these people with some form of intelligence and to get it so wrong for so long. Irish Democracy is a non starter, first of all we were ruled by the British, then by the Catholic Church and, latterly and to the present day, by Germany, France and Brussels. I often wonder if the Irish people would ever wake up, or as I suspect we have been downtrodden for so many hundreds of years that it has gotten into the genes of generation after generation, and that I believe is what I call the sheep mentally. Oh its so easy for the Bureaucrats to rule our country never questioning always believing what one reads in the press and if its on R.T.E. the National Television Station well its better than the bible. I sometimes think of what would happen if they gave a vote to all of the emigrants, what with their different reasons for having to leave their country and how they now feel about things, a visit home at Christmas, a few

A Prison sentence, Crime, Mother died aged twenty eight

letters, and the odd phone call, the dream of making a fortune and say in maybe 10 years to make enough to go home and start your own business, as I said the more things change the more things stay the same.

In 1995 the birth rate has been falling for the last number of years, I believe it has halved to around 50,000 maybe if this continues for another few years we may have no unemployment problem, I wonder which political party will take credit for this?

A Prisoner, But What Crime?

One sunny morning I think it was early spring we were walked from a house, which we had been staying, in with some lady, I cannot recall her name because sometime earlier our own house at St. Anthony's Road was repossessed for non payment of rent to the Cork Court House. I have only a vague recollection of this event but I'm sure it must have been quite frightening. From there we were taken to Greenmount, I think it was called a Reformatory School you know for delinquent boys, boys who maybe stole, and were constantly misbehaving. We, myself, and my brothers had broken no law, why we were imprisoned in a reformatory school I still don't know. Things were not so bad in Greenmount, the food was bad but a little wicker gate was left open so the boys could go down to Barrack Street, to buy sweets and swap comics. Saturday's were really special because we were taken to the pictures. We were given a choice, I believe the way it worked was that the older boys went to the Savoy, the next went to the Palace, and the youngest went to the Capital Cinema, you must remember that going to the cinema was a real treat in those day's, and a big occasion for most people as television would not be seen in Ireland for another few years yet. Sometimes people sitting near us would know that we were from Greenmount and share their sweets with us. I believe I was the youngest boy in Greenmount and made my First Communion there. The reason I remember it so well is not because of my clothing well more my shoes, let me explain, as the days got closer I had got a suit from the Monks but on the morning of my Communion they gave me a pair of shoes with straps on them. I

FORM X.

AN CHUIRT DUITHCHE
(THE DISTRICT COURT)

No. 144.

CHILDREN ACTS, 1908 TO 1941

Order of Detention in a Certified Industrial School

Inspr W O'Callaghan
I S P P C .... Complainant | District Court Area of ...... **Cork** ....

.... Thomas Cronin .... Defendant | District No. .... **2v** ....

(1) Insert here the appropriate recital from Part II of the District Court Rules, 1942. (No. 2).

WHEREAS (1) Thomas Cronin who appears to the court to a child under the age of fifteen years having been born so far as has been ascertained on the 18th day of April 1951 and who resides at 41 St Anthonys Road Gurranabraher Cork in the County Borough of Cork, has been found having a parent who does not exercise proper guardianship

(2) Delete the word "borough" where not required.

AND WHEREAS THE COUNCIL OF THE SAID COUNTY (2) BOROUGH HAS BEEN GIVEN AN OPPORTUNITY OF BEING HEARD

AND WHEREAS THE COURT IS SATISFIED THAT IT IS EXPEDIENT TO DEAL WITH THE SAID CHILD BY SENDING HIM TO A CERTIFIED INDUSTRIAL SCHOOL.

AND WHEREAS THE RELIGIOUS PERSUASION OF THE SAID CHILD APPEARS TO THE COURT TO BE CATHOLIC.

IT IS HEREBY ORDERED THAT THE SAID CHILD SHALL BE SENT TO THE

CERTIFIED INDUSTRIAL SCHOOL AT **Greenmount Cork** , BEING A SCHOOL

CONDUCTED IN ACCORDANCE WITH THE DOCTRINES OF THE CATHOLIC CHURCH, THE

MANAGERS WHEREOF ARE WILLING TO RECEIVE HIM TO BE THERE DETAINED UNTIL,

(3) Insert date up to but not including which detention is to continue

BUT NOT INCLUDING (3) THE 18th DAY OF **April** , 1967

AND IT IS FURTHER ORDERED THAT RESIDING

(4) Insert "parent of" or "person legally liable to maintain."

AT THE (4)

THE SAID CHILD SHALL PAY TO THE INSPECTOR OF REFORMATORY AND INDUSTRIAL

(5) Insert "during the whole of the time for which the said child is liable to be detained in the school" or "until further order."

SCHOOLS A WEEKLY SUM OF SHILLINGS (5)

THE FIRST PAYMENT TO BE MADE ON THE DAY OF

GIVEN UNDER MY HAND, THIS 2nd DAY OF June , 19 58

Denis O'Donovan.

JUSTICE OF THE DISTRICT COURT ASSIGNED
TO SAID DISTRICT.

1-2198-G.20A.3000.11/55.D.(D.P.B.)Ltd.

21/12/59 by O/m '67

This piece of paper gives me a prison sentence and record for nine years.
Crime: Mother died
Age: Seven years

remember crying and getting very upset, until eventually the brothers come up with another pair of shoes which were about two or three sizes too big for me.

I was quite happy with them, and wore them on my communion day. Oh one other thing, I remember going into Woolworth's and buying a dinky, where I got the money I don't know. Unlike most children who make their communion in Ireland, most can tell how much money they "make" and there is great excitement among all of the children to find out who has made the most money. This was not a problem for me. I have wondered if this could be one of the reasons why Religion has never played a large part of my life, because even as a young child religion and the system had begun to fail me.

Christmas was coming and the goose was getting fat or so we were told, new shoes, turkey something you could only dream about from one end of the year to the next now it was countdown time, 8,7,6,5 weeks to go and so on until at last it was Christmas week. I'm sure every Boy or Girl who grew up in those years, will have known the threats that would have been made by their parents, whether it was Johnny "if you don't behave Santa will not bring you a new bike, or Mary if you don't do your chores Santa will give your doll to Dolores next door" and so on. My brothers and I did not even have the pleasure of these threats made against us. How I have cursed this Santa who only comes to good children, I had only been on this earth maybe six years and the amount of kindness I had seen lets say I wasn't overwhelmed. Maybe this Christmas, Santa would really come to me but already I was starting to have my doubts, I now look back and feel cheated that my childhood was taken from me before it even started or maybe I was brought into the real world sooner than most children.

My Christmas Family

A few days before Christmas of that year one of the monks approached me and asked if I would like to spend Christmas with a family. I believe a lot if not most of the boys were going home to their parents for the Christmas period, I did not hesitate "Oh yes, brother I would be very happy to go to a real family and spend Christmas with them", what the hell I had nothing to lose and at least I would be somewhat free for a little while. Its amazing to look back now and see that I was beginning to think like a little caged animal, so young and yet my outlook on life was being formed by the treatment I was receiving from my peers. The family arrived and low and behold they had a car from what I remember, it was a Black Ford, this was the second time I had ridden in a car, at least it was a little bit happier for me. They had 2 children, a boy and a girl and a big fluffy dog. That family could not have been nicer to me, I still to this day wonder about them, the parents must now I'm sure, be dead, the children must be married, and probably have grown children of their own. I can honestly say it was my most happiest Christmas ever as a child, I don't even know these folks names yet the kindness that they showed me has never been forgotten, it was I believe the first bit of real kindness that had been shown to me. For the very first time not only did I see a plum pudding and they actually caught it on fire, at the time I stood wide eyed and mesmerized by this wonderful sight, and best of all then, we ate it. I played with their dog, ate their food, played with the boy and girl, and for a few days became part of a family.

I can still remember how good it felt, and I do remember the lady asking me on more than one occasion if I would like to live with them on a permanent basis. Of course I said yes, she said they would try and do something about it. I do believe now that they tried to adopt me but with my father still living this was not possible mores the pity with a little bit of good luck I might have had a nice childhood after all. But alas good luck and me were never companions. All too soon my Christmas holiday, came to an end. I remember been driven back to Greenmount very late at night, with lots of presents saying goodbye to my family. They promised that they would take me out again but I think the pain of not being able to take me home with them permanently, was too much for them. Whenever Christmas comes around I think of them and the plum pudding. I think of them fondly, and always remember their kindness and thank them for at least one happy Christmas.

The Opera House Burning

One December evening in 1955 there was great excitement we were all drawn to the windows of our house, from this advantage point we

OPERA HOUSE AND SCHOOL OF ART, CORK.

The Cork Opera House in all its splendor
(*picture courtesy Michael Lenihan*)

could all see a huge fire with the flames reaching high into the late evening sky. It was the Cork Opera House, a beautiful building by all accounts so I was told, never having had the pleasure of being a patron. We watched the fire for what seemed like hours and you know when you are a child fire has a certain fascination. The whole of Cork City must have shed a tear that night, it was to be many years later before Cork City was to get another Opera House, and having seen the photo's of the Old one and spoken to other older people who were regular patrons there was no contest between the two buildings.

The Closing of Greenmount

There was big excitement for about a week, rumour and counter rumour, Greenmount was closing down, no it was not we were never told the truth, but one morning we were told that we were going on a picnic. Jesus some picnic, we all trotted happily along to a line of waiting buses, and now in hindsight I remember some people waiting around and giving some of the boy's sweets not much for a six year old to think about, a picnic sounded good to me, I was happy its true what they say, ignorance is bliss.

All too soon we arrived at Upton, we still did not know where we were, well at least I didn't, and when we were told to form single lines and one of the boys did not respond he got a clatter from a Christian Brother that sent him sprawling across the yard. The rumour then went out that we were only there for a day, fat chance. To say that Upton was one of the most hideous places that I ever had the misfortune to be detained in, would be an understatement. Me and my brother's crime was having no parents. I do believe somewhere in the Irish Constitution it states that all the children will be treated equally, that certainly did not happen to me, and I'm sure there were and still are many more. Past and present Politicians and Clergy, hang your heads in shame.

Breakfast, 3 slices of bread with dripping on them, Porridge with Salt and Dinner some Swill, and something that resembled potatoes, I can remember being so hungry one evening that I eat a dessert spoonful of Salt that's hunger. I did not know what the Christian Brothers were I knew they were something, I now know they were sadists of the worst type, they must have been frustrated decrepit old bastards, and if there is a hell I hope they are still burning. In the summer time they used to hire us out to the farmers to pick their potatoes and I think they used to pay us about 5D that's about 2p today, but you would not see the money, but would be credited with it to spend at their shop, no don't go getting the wrong idea the shop, consisted of some 1p bars and sweets 6 for a penny. After we were finished a days work we would burn all of the leaves etc. and this was our chance to put some potatoes into the fire, so that they may roast if you were lucky, you might get one but I can remember eating them raw. Corporal punishment is now outlawed, not before time, if for instance you had a hole in your stocking you would be brought into the office and made to bend over a stool and given three lashes with a 12 inch long leather strap across the backside, this was regarded as punishment. The same would apply for wetting your bed, which consisted of a mattress on a slatted base. On another occasion three of the older lads decided they would run away and try to get back home to Dublin. I believe that when they were caught after one or two days, that they were first lashed, then all their hair was shaved off and they were marched around the yard as a spectacle to all the other lads so that no one would try the same thing.

The Sadist

Brother Johnson was a big bully of a "Man" or that's how I remember him. One morning I remember him with a shotgun and shooting some Crows that had built their nest in some trees outside the schoolyard. On other occasions he used to go shooting, he had two gun dogs but alas I don't think he used them, because he used to take some lads with him as well, when he had shot something he would force the lads to go and fetch whatever it was, that meant going through brambles, across streams etc, so in other words the lads were doing what the dogs were supposed to be doing and may God help them if they did not return with whatever it was that he shot. This is just one of the stories I'm sure that there are many more I know to be true.

Bath Time

Saturday Mornings was the time allocated to having a bath. If my memory has served me right they were long troughs, in which you could either stand or sit to wash yourself. One particular Saturday Morning I washed myself as usual when I went to the centre of the washroom where a monk was standing, he would inspect each boy as he came out of the troughs, there must have been a little dirt behind my ears which I had failed to wash, he hit me such a punch that he knocked me from the centre of the baths right back into the trough. You must remember I was seven or eight years of age at the time. I was either the youngest or the second youngest in the place so to say that I found it very intimidating and frightening is an understatement and before too long any confidence you may have had would be long gone, replaced by fear and insecurity, which in my case has remained with me all of my life.

The Dentist

One day in Autumn the dentist came to Upton, it was late afternoon when my turn came, I may have had one tooth that needed attention, in any event he pulled 5 or 6, I remember him saying that they were milk teeth so it was just as well to take them all out. I came out of the room in a daze, I must have been crying with pain but I had to sit on the bench in the yard in the cold with my mouth full of blood for about 2 hours until they opened the dormitory I could safely say I did not have my supper that night. These are just a few of the things that I remember about this horrible place, thankfully myself and my brothers only spent about 1 year at that place but even that period of time was too long and I know that it has clouded my outlook on life in general. I often think that if I had to spend 7 or 8 years there until I was sixteen, like I'm sure a lot of the boys had to, I'm afraid to think what would have become of me. I believe I escaped just in time and thankfully they did not break my spirit, by Jesus, they had a good try. I know that there were other boys who were not so lucky.

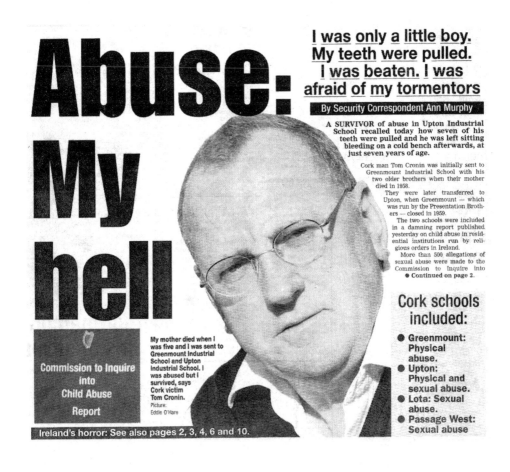

Abuse: My hell

I was only a little boy. My teeth were pulled. I was beaten. I was afraid of my tormentors

By Security Correspondent Ann Murphy

A SURVIVOR of abuse in Upton Industrial School recalled today how seven of his teeth were pulled and he was left sitting bleeding on a cold bench afterwards, at just seven years of age.

Cork man Tom Cronin was initially sent to Greenmount Industrial School with his two older brothers when their mother died in 1958.

They were later transferred to Upton, when Greenmount — which was run by the Presentation Brothers — closed in 1959.

The two schools were included in a damning report published yesterday on child abuse in residential institutions run by religious orders in Ireland.

More than 500 allegations of sexual abuse were made to the Commission to Inquire into

● Continued on page 2.

● Continued on page 2.

Cork schools included:

● **Greenmount: Physical abuse.**
● **Upton: Physical and sexual abuse.**
● **Lota: Sexual abuse.**
● **Passage West: Sexual abuse**

Commission to Inquire into Child Abuse Report

My mother died when I was five and I was sent to Greenmount Industrial School and Upton Industrial School. I was abused but I survived, says Cork victim Tom Cronin.

Picture: Eddie O'Hare

Ireland's horror: See also pages 2, 3, 4, 6 and 10.

Words alone could never describe the horrors of these hell holes

Horrific scale of abuse makes headlines in world press

by Noel Baker

THE horrific scale of the abuse carried out against children made headlines around the world.

Major media organisations carried news of the findings of the Commission to Inquire into Child Abuse and, in some countries, there were calls for similar investigations into alleged abuses there.

The Sydney Morning Herald reported how the report into "endemic" child abuse in church institutions in Ireland has sparked fresh calls for a royal commission into historical child abuse in Australia.

"Victims' groups say the culture of abuse in Catholic institutions here last century could have been as shocking as what is revealed in the nine-year Irish commission's report, and that as many as one in 10 priests, brothers and nuns could have a case to answer for sexual, emotional or physical abuse."

It added that 12 of the 1,090 witnesses interviewed for the report now live in Australia and New Zealand, amid estimates that 4% of Irish victims moved there, along with "an unknown number of alleged perpetrators".

Time.com reported: "As well as documenting the most depraved acts committed by school staff, Justice Sean Ryan's report condemns the culture of secrecy that prevailed in the institutions. Incidents of child abuse committed by members of religious orders were almost never reported to the police. Furthermore, priests who were known abusers were often transferred to other institutions where they continued to abuse children."

The Toronto Star reported how "Irish children lived with terror'", while the New York Times car-

The New York Times carried the abuse report on its front page.

ried the views of victims' groups in America.

"David Clohessy, director of the Survivors Network of Those Abused by Priests, a group based in St Louis, said that, while the report had failed in its duty to bring the perpetrators to justice, it had been clear about the failings of the church," said the paper.

"Terence McKiernan, president of BishopAccountability.org, an American group that maintains an internet archive of material related to Catholic abuse, said that the report had failed by not going far enough."

In France, Le Monde noted how after five volumes, 2,600 pages, and nine years of inquiry, there was one definitive result: that priests and monks beat and raped children in 216 Catholic institutions.

In Germany, newspaper Sueddeutsche Zeitung carried a report on the findings under the easy-to-translate headline: 'Häuser des Horrors'.

Ireland's image as the 'Island of Saints and Scholars' is damaged beyond repair

My hell at hands of Cork's abusive Brothers

Known paedophile one of seven abusers at Upton

1,100 tell their story of abuse to report committee

By ANN MURPHY
Security Correspondent

From page one.
Child Abuse, chaired by Justice Seán Ryan.
The report also contains details of horrendous physical abuse suffered by residents of the institutions.
Tom Cronin recalled today how he was beaten in Greenmount but described Upton, where he also spent 18 months, as hell.
He said: "There was one occasion when a dentist was brought in and pulled seven of my milk teeth. I was left sitting in the cold with blood coming out of my mouth for a while until the dormitory was opened."
He added: "I got beaten with a leather strap at five years old if my boots were not cleaned properly."
He said he has lived a nomadic lifestyle as an

THE Commission to Inquire into Child Abuse was set up in 2000, under its first chairwoman, Justice Mary Laffoy.
The chairman who oversaw the report issued yesterday was Justice Seán Ryan.
Its three functions were:
● To hear evidence of

THE Rosminian industrial school in Upton was set up in the late 1800s and closed in 1966.
The report summary reads: "Included in the documents discovered by the Rosminians were two Punishment Books for this school. One related to the 1889-1893 period and the other related to the period 1952 – 1963. This latter book contained clear documentary evidence of a harsh regime in Upton. The Order conceded that punishment was abusive and at times brutal."
It continued: "The issue of sexual abuse in this institution emerged most strikingly through material that came to the Investigation Committee's attention following a search by the Order of material in their archive in Rome, which disclosed a considerable number of documents, 68 in all, dating from 1936 to 1968. They dealt with, among other things, seven sexual abusers who worked in Upton."
The report said that these documents provided a valuable contemporary account of how sexual abuse was dealt with.

UPTON

beatings were also administered."
One witness said he was resident in Upton from the early 1960s and the daily routine often involved receiving a smack on the face for minor things.
Another witness recalled hearing the screams and cries of other boys after they were taken from their beds to the office for punishment in the evenings. Two other witnesses gave up to 150 boys were beaten after clapping at the end of a film they were shown.
Seven sexual abusers worked in Upton between 1936 and 1968. The report said: "Respondent evidence and the Rosminian survey disclosed that sexual abuse perpetrated by a lay teacher and employees in the Institution had been discovered and was dealt with through the removal or transfer of the offenders.. It is clear, however, that a large number of the perpetrators of the abuse were discovered as a result of the activities of Br Alfonso, who pursued a policy

The Government and the Catholic Church can no longer deny that it ever happened

Eilish O'Regan
Health Correspondent

SUFFER the little children, particularly it seems the most vulnerable.

The Ryan report found children with bad hearing, eyesight or learning difficulties were particularly vulnerable to sexual abuse.

The confidential committee heard 59 reports of abuse from 58 witnesses, 39 male and 19 female, relating to 14 special needs schools and residential services managed by religious congregations.

They frequently had to travel far from home and live in residential care to get the treatment they needed.

Witnesses reported that while attending special needs services they were physically abused and assaulted using leather straps, canes, spade and broom handles, kitchen implements and rulers.

Gagged

People in three different facilities reported being taken from their beds at night by male religious staff and sexually abused by a staff member.

In some cases, physical violence accompanied sexual abuse and victims recalled having their heads held under water, being bound and gagged and otherwise restrained.

Two were assaulted by "gangs" of fellow residents.

One was brought to a pub

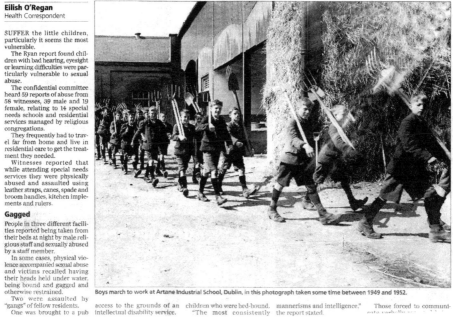

Boys march to work at Artane Industrial School, Dublin, in this photograph taken some time between 1949 and 1952.

access to the grounds of an intellectual disability service.

children who were bed-bound. "The most consistently

mannerisms and intelligence." the report stated.

Those forced to communi-

Schooling, what's that?

23

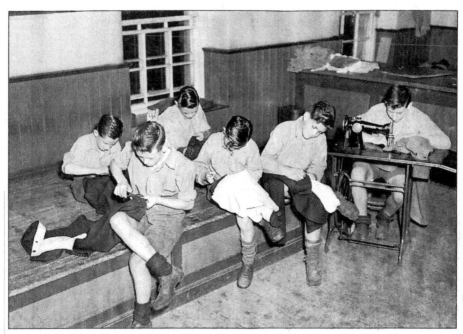

St Patrick's, Upton, Co Cork. Work was a central feature of daily life, both indoor and outdoor, including weaving, carpentry and farm work.

Slave labour was the order of the day

EVENING ECHO, Thursday, May 21, 2009

NEWS

AND GREENMOUNT REVEALED AS NATION REELS AT REPORT INTO INDUSTRIAL SCHOOL ABUSES

Cork school: Naked children tied to ladder and whipped

GREENMOUNT Industrial School in Cork city which was owned and managed by the Presentation Brothers is dealt with in the fourth chapter of the child abuse report.

This school was founded in 1874 and closed in 1959. It was certified for 235 boys.

The report summary said: "For some specific periods during its history, Greenmount operated a harsh and severe regime.

"The level of corporal punishment tolerated depended on the attitude of management at the time.

"Some Resident Managers were more severe than others."

It continued: "The report into Greenmount contains a detailed analysis of an investigation into allegations of sexual abuse against two Brothers who were on the staff at the time.

"This matter was dealt with inadequately at the time and one of the Brothers went on to abuse in other schools he was assigned to."

The report found that food, cloth-

GREENMOUNT

aftercare were badly provided.

In 2004, the Vice Principal of the Presentation Anglo Irish Province, Brother Denis Minehane, spoke to the Commission in relation to Greenmount.

He said: "We have not formed a view that systematic child abuse occurred at Greenmount Industrial School.

"We are prepared to accept that a harsh regime operated there which would be unacceptable by today's standards."

The report outlined that the Presentation Brothers conceded that a harsh regime existed in Greenmount, especially in the 1940s. It added: "The corporal punishment administered by the Superior, Brother Arrio, during the 1940s was excessive."

One of the complainants referred to Brother Arrio as a tyrant.

He continued: "He took pleasure, and it helped him in some sick, sadistic way to beat children, and he had his own ways of doing it.

Greenmount Industrial School sports in 1928: "For some periods during its history, Greenmount operated a harsh and severe regime."

commonly known in Greenmount School as "up the ladder". That will never leave my memory."

He continued: "You stood on — that type of ladder ... and you were naked, which was a horror thing for any man saying he was a member of religion or knew there was a God there or recognised a God, as a child you are up there hanging on to

"That's when he lashed you across the buttocks, the hips or maybe the raw thighs.

"And the way he left you, you were given a white nicks like a footballer and you wore that for many days, all dressed up and the boys could laugh at you, but on top of that you had to go to the nurse and get iodine on it."

punishment administered by this Brother was contrary to the Rules and Regulations for Certified Industrial Schools and was severe by the standards of this time.

"There was no system in place to control his excesses."

It added: "The misleading nature of the annual reports to the Department of Education indicated knowledge on the part of the authorities that what they were doing was wrong."

The report outlined that the Resident Manager Brother Carlito (a pseudonym) and a senior teaching staff member, Brother Garcia, were the subject of allegations of sexual abuse in 1965.

The report concluded: "It is not clear that the investigation in 1955 established that the Brothers were guilty of the charges made against them."

It added that although the then bishop and his senior clerical investigator believed they had engaged in sexual abuse, the two men were permitted to move on to new positions dealing with children.

Sexual abuse between boys, and

Greenmount Industrial School Cork
A harsh and severe regime operated at this place

Schoolboys in a physical training class in the Greenmount Industrial School yard 26/10/37. Below: Schoolboys helping with the harvest 02/08/1934.

These schools were prisons for children

Bang, Bang, Bang, Cronin Wake Up, Wake Up, you're on Watch in half an hour. I shot up straight in my bunk; sweat dripping from my forehead my body, drenched in sweat. I began to realise where I was, as I got dressed and ready I thought of my dream, no it was neither a dream nor a nightmare. I then realised I had not been asleep at all just somewhere back in my youth, somewhere real yet now somewhat detached I wondered if the human brain sometimes can do this, you know if something proves to be too hurtful to remember there is something built in to make us shut off, or at least make it seem distant to us so as not to feel all of the pain. I closed the door to my Cabin and hoped I had also closed the dark door to my wretched Childhood.

CHAPTER THREE

Churchfield

After what seemed like a lifetime some sort of a deal was done between a woman, who had years earlier lived with us for a little while with her daughter, after our mother died, and before we had been placed in Greenmount. She looked after the house, cooking etc, then I believe she got her own house at Churchfield and left, anyway unknown to us Mrs O'Callaghan, Nora as we called her and her daughter wanted to bring us to her house in Churchfield, and eventually she became our guardian, we were released into her care. I remember that time vividly, my father came in a van to collect us, and only now when I think back as to how the other lads must have felt, anyway I was so glad to be getting out, I did not give it much thought and as I say we did not spend a long time in Upton but it has haunted me all my life. On the journey home I remember that we stopped at a pub, how could my father go anywhere without drink, we got to Churchfield sometime around midnight and for years I believed that Upton was many miles from Cork, not just the 15 or so that it really is. The early days at Churchfield Gardens were fairly uneventful, we were enrolled in a new school, Blarney Street CBS. Run by the Christian Brothers. Nora's Husband Christy was an ex Army Man, and he and Nora did not have a very good marriage, they seldom talked or spoke to one another, they slept in separate rooms, and Nora was constantly given out about him, Eileen, Nora's daughter did not have much to say to Christy either, and very soon a pecking order developed in the house, Eileen came first followed by my eldest brother John, I think I came next with my brother Paul, in the bottom or maybe bottom spot swapped between my brother Paul, and myself. We had regained our freedom, but at what price, there was no happiness in Churchfield so it was up to ourselves to grab whatever we could.

On the Buses

Come On Tommy, I'll get you on, Come On, Run Faster, it was Junior Ryan, one of the lads from Churchfield Gardens, it was 12:15 midweek, and we were on our way home from school for our midday lunch, whatever that meant he was swinging from the back of a single decked bus, which in these days had a ladder up the centre of the back. My heart started to beat and pound should I do it? It was beginning to pull away from the bus stop come on Tommy run, I was just 20 feet away, my heart took over from my brain and run I did, well what a thrill Junior grabbed me and swung me inside him and then straddled me with his legs, we were on our way courtesy of the C.I.E. and free of charge, it was Magic, I had tasted my first thrill in life. I soon became an expert at hanging on to buses, or indeed for that matter any other type of lorry, be it Coal truck, which was my least favourite or brewery lorry, even though the buses were my favourite they were nearly my downfall, let me explain, I became so expert that I used to go to a bus stop which was well out of my way home, but perused a longer spin, on one particular day I was looking into a toy shop waiting for my bus, turning around I spotted it coming and without looking ran straight across the road and into a motorbike, straight up in the air and down again, I landed with a thump, the Motorcyclist asked me if I was alright, yes sir says I, picking myself up gingerly from the ground, by this time a crowd had started to gather, again the man asked me if I was alright, will I call a Guard? Oh no sir, I'm fine, and with that I slank away and headed for home.

Thankfully there were no broken bones, however I had a lot of cuts and skin burn on my thighs, I dare not tell Nora what had happened to me, in the first instance I should not have been at that particular spot and she was not a very sympathetic person. It healed before too long and very soon I was back on the buses. On another occasion I was on the roof of the bus lying down on my back looking up at the sky and singing, some one shouted, Squad Car and on looking up sure enough there was a Police Car coming up behind us, as the bus came to a halt I jumped from the roof and on landing started to run, however my legs would not respond as I knew they should, I was caught fairly quickly by a Garda who took my name and address and told me I would be getting a summons, you can imagine how I felt, worst was to follow, my two ankles began to swell at once and after a few hours I had to tell Nora as when I took my shoes off I could not get them on again. I had sprained both my ankles. The Guards did not summons me on that occasion maybe they felt I suffered enough. On one other time I again was caught by the Garda this time hanging from a Coal Lorry and when I was called to court I was fined 5 shillings which was a lot of money in those days, I must have got a hiding because I don't remember hanging on much after that. I do remember also at that time one lad got knocked down and was killed. I think that cured a lot of us. Just remembering about shoes brings me to my shoe situation, whenever I got a new pair of shoes which was all too seldom, within a short time the shoes would wear, when this happened we would have to get some cardboard and slot it over the hole which would be getting bigger on a daily basis if it rained the cardboard would not work long even if it stayed fine it would wear away soon. Now if you were on your own it wouldn't be so bad because you could watch out for glass or nails etc. and take evasive action, but if you were with some of your friends you could not go skipping and dodging around the footpath, so you would have to endure the pain of a sliver of glass or a little stone or pebbles or what ever you would think that with all of that body swerving I should have been a great footballer.

Mrs Cronin

Mrs. Cronin and her family lived at No 8 Churchfield Gardens, and even though she had a large family herself she was always giving us something, like she would call me and say something like, Tommy my Sean has grown too big for these shoes see if they will fit you, and more often than not they would be perfect she was always handing in food saying she had cooked too much and nobody would eat it, bless her heart. Mrs Fermore at No. 6 was just as kind and I do believe that she cooked on some days especially for us, there would be a tap on the back door and a stew would be handed over, such generosity and kindness should not go unrewarded, however I do believe their happiness was in the giving. Mrs Fermore and her family were good to us.

After School

After the School day finished before we wound our way home there would eventually be some fight to be won or lost we would go to a garden of a big disused haunted house in the vicinity of Blarney Street, it went by the name of Mona's, Hold me sack, I'm going to kill him and so with a large circle of lads gathered around the fight would end before any damage was done some bright spark would shout something like look out its Mona, and with that there would be a scatter and all of the fighting would be forgotten for another day, the best thing was that nobody lost face and both parties would say that they would have won, if it had not been called off.

Fishing

In the summertime and especially during our holidays one of the things we used to do was go under one of the bridges spanning the River Lee and Stracall that is, with an illegal hook catch. Mullet which we would endeavour to sell to some Fish Merchant for as we were told they were then sold to Dublin Zoo for food for the seals. One particular evening we had been fishing as usual, and before we knew it the tide had started to come in. I was last to make my way up and the final part of the climb was to scale at nearly right angles to the bridge along a length of steel. When I got to the end of it my legs were dangling just above the water and I was hanging on for dear life. I could not get my legs to swing up far enough to pull myself up and my arms were beginning to tire, I was now quite frightened and my companions could not help me just then my eldest brother happened to come along I think he was a messenger boy at the time, he swung over the rail grabbed my jumper and hauled me up by the neck, when he got me safely on the Bridge he pasted me and gave me a good hiding, I was so glad to be alive I did not mind and it seemed like a small price to pay.

My Working Life Begins

When I reached 10 or 11, I got the job that my two brothers had done before me. After school on Wednesday, and Friday, I would go to Reardon's Restaurant, on Merchants Quay to take all the laundry to Mc Curtain Street Laundrette, put it through the Machines and return it to Reardon's, where I would be sat down to a dinner of Chips, Sausages, and Tea, Sweets and Cakes, on finishing, and before I left I would be given two and six, so that was Five Shillings per week, I think I used to hand up most of it, if not all of it, still it was good training for me, and got me into the workplace very early on. After I got too old for Reardon's Laundry. I guess I was around 12 years old I got a job in a shop called the Plunkett Fruit Stores, which was situated at the top of Oliver Plunkett Street, it was every day after school and all day Saturday so, at 12 years, I was a part-time Messenger Boy, the wages were 30 Shillings or £1.50 in today's terms. The days of going to see the fights or getting up to mischief were now gone because we were left out of school at 4pm and I would have to go into town to be in the shop at five past. I would then be given the deliveries, potatoes here, carrots and turnips there, and so it went until all the deliveries were finished for that day. The shop was owned by two ladies they must be dead now as they seemed quite old to me at the time. The messenger bike I had was of the type known by all of the messengers as the tank, because of construction and to have a few stone of potatoes, as well as veg in your front basket to try and push that bike up one of the steep hills of Cork took some doing. I remember at that time there was a group of Shops in Cork called the Economy Shops, they were butchers and they had a string of messenger boys, this job in particular was known as very hard, you could often hear the lads calling out to one another, Sham, who are you working for, back came the reply, the Economy Shops, that's a horses job boy, O Fuck Off, and then a threat would be issued, I'll fucking catch you tomorrow, not on that tank you wont, and off they would go on their merry ways passing each other like ships in the night, other times you could hear them calling each other in Patrick Street, Paddy, Sean, or whatever, where are you going boy? Douglas. Where are you off to? Western Road, Come on to Douglas with me and I will go to the Western Rd, with you when I'm finished. I can't boy, I'll be sacked, come on I have only a few deliveries to make, let you come to the Western Rd with me first, go away and fuck yourself, you must think I'm stupid, you'll shoot back into town, just then another messenger boy would happen along "hey I'm going to Douglas" lets go, I'll be out all the way with ye, that's great boy. It was hard enough to pedal these bikes normally but when it rained you were issued with a set of Oilskins, and a hat not the lightweight gear that you get today, but real heavy stuff. A perk of the job was being left to take the bike home on Sunday, but big trouble for you if anything happened to that bike not that as I've already said that was likely to happen, as they were built like tanks. My ambition at this point was to progress to a bike without a basket, in other words a normal bike, jobs with ordinary bikes were at J.R. Barry's a Ladies Retail Shop very upmarket in Patrick Street. I was now the crème de le crème of the messenger boy fraternity, I was working in a high class shop and had a normal bike with just a small basket on the front and I believe the wages were better along with this, when I delivered the dress or the coat or whatever I would usually get a tip. Then on quiet days one of the ladies that worked in the shop would need some message doing and when I returned they would normally tell me to keep the change, which might be 2 shilling or 2 in 6, if it was pay day you might get more. I remember about this time as well there was a messenger boy strike, they were looking for a rise from £2-5 to 2-10 which I believe they got however one of the things I remember about the strike is that any messenger boy caught working his bike would have been taken from him and thrown into the River Lee. I was not very long at my job at J. R. Barry's, when one evening Mr Barry told me to go to the Munster Cycle Shop and get a new bike. Well I was overjoyed, especially as I did not think that there was not a lot wrong with the old one. The Munster Cycle Co. was owned by two English Gentlemen and when they sorted out my new bike I was in for another surprise as they gave me 5 Shillings for myself what a great way to do business I still remember that 5 Shillings maybe some of today's Business People could learn something from this. When it was quiet at

J.R. Barry's I would go to the stores and flatten some cardboard boxes and take them to the Waste Paper factory, where on weighing them you would be given a ticket to take to the cash office where you would be paid, usually around 9d which would buy milk and cakes, or fags, which you could buy loose for 2d each. I had collected Waste Paper during my summer holidays before I had got a proper job myself, and sometimes a friend would go to the Waste Paper Factory and collect some empty sacks, we would then proceed to go from shop to shop asking if they had any waste paper, if we were lucky we would fill up and go back to the Waste Paper Factory, get some money and go out again after a hard day we would start buying crisps, maybe a bag of chips, because collecting waste paper is a very hungry pastime. On certain occasions if the waste paper we had collected was not very heavy we would get a heavy rock, and place it very carefully in the centre of the sack surrounded by the paper, this was a very dangerous thing to do because if we were caught we would be barred from the Waste Paper Factory we were never caught, and did not have to stoop to this level of dishonesty very often.

Going to the Cinema? Dream On

Summertime and the living is easy O Yah! Dream on boy. The Lido, or the Assemb's or to give it it's proper name The Assembly Room's these were the two Picture Houses "Cinema's" we aspired to and come hell or high water we had to get to money for this entertainment. 4D old pennies in the case of the Lido and one Shilling in the case of the Assemb's, Batman and Robin, off the cliff, next week, Billy the Kid, Bang Bang your dead, Tarzan and the rest. The Usher in the Assemb's was called George, when someone was shot on the Big Screen a shout would go up remove the body George, he would then start flashing his torch to see if he could catch someone, it's funny how things like this stick in our memories forever, and more important things at times escape us.

The Lido boy it was better than Lourdes, you could go in there crippled and come out walking, O yeah, with fleas? The other cinemas in Cork, The Capital, The Savoy, The Palace, they were all too expensive for us. So Sunday night on our patch was a big night, all of the boy's would meet under a certain street light, and after some messing, spitting at each other hitting,. and pissing, on one another we would get down to business. What's happening in the morning boy's? Well Christy, what the fuck are you up to tomorrow. O I'm going collecting Scrap Metal with so and so, what are you doing Jim? Messenger Boy in the English Market an Uncle of mine put a word in for me, the regular boy is on holiday, and I can take the bike home at night, someone gave him a kick and called him a lucky bastard. And so it went until those that were left had little or no option but to suggest collecting Waste Paper. Oh no not Waste Paper, the worst of ways to try and make a few shillings if we were lucky. The king of Waste Paper collection on our patch was a lad by the name of Pat Monaghan, Pat old friend, buddy, how's about me teaming up with you tomorrow I'll do all the donkey work, Pat was so well known that he had all his own contacts that used to keep the paper for him. Oh no, I'm going on my own, a privilege a great gesture, if you were brought along to collect Waste Paper with Pat Monaghan, and nothing else would ever again eclipse this event if you were lucky. For once my luck was in, O.K. call me in the morning at 9am ,and don't be fucking late or I'm gone. Yes Pat, Yes Pat, he must be going soft in the head.

My friend at that time was a boy by the name of Michael Coleman. Michael was a Messenger Boy. Now Michael had a bike, the deal was if I went with him on his errands I could use his bike, it seems so stupid now but back then it seemed a grand thing, amazing that what seems most important at certain times, in the past, pales into insignificance, nothing, it really didn't matter at all.

Work – a hiding – what next?

Looking back now and maybe I'm seeing things through rose tinted glasses this period seemed like a happy time for me. Maybe it was, I had a lot of freedom, I was working and making some money. It must have done my confidence a world of good, I did have other messenger boy jobs, one in particular sticks out in my mind, it was a garage called P.J 0'Hea's on Patrick's Quay in Cork. One of my duties was to go to City Hall and tax any new car that was sold. One day about 12:30 one of the staff asked me to hurry and go to the Tax Offices, I pointed out to him that I did not have a bike and so would not make it before they closed. He pointed to a bike nearby, told me to take it, so away I went, it was just gone 1pm. When I returned it the man that told me to take the bike was standing at the door with another man a mechanic that worked in the garage as I got off the bike, I went to hand it to the mechanic but as I done so he hit me a stunning blow to the face, with that I threw the bike at him and went into my pocket where I had a penknife, with this he went berserk, threw me to the ground and proceeded to knock my head against the footpath, you must remember this man was about 24 years old, where as I was maybe at the most 15 years old, anyway a Guard happened to pass along, at this stage I was half unconscious, the mechanic told his side of the story, saying that I had stolen his bike, the man who told me to take the bike saw everything that was happening but failed to act in my favour, the Guards reply was that he hadn't hit me hard enough. I'm sure he damaged my brain that day. Many years later I happened to be passing the Garage and went in to see if my mechanic was still working there, but alas I could not find him, maybe it's just as well. About this time I also worked as a Plumber's Mate, for those who don't know what that is let me explain. In those day's if your Father was a painter, then you would become a painter and so on, in other words the Unions were very strong and try as I might I could not become a plumber, the best I could hope for was a Plumbers Mate, whose duties included carrying the plumbers tools, helping him with his tools, going back to the stores if he needed any supplies, and making tea. I particularly liked this I found it interesting and every job was different, for instance it could be a broken pipe, or a blocked drain, or fitting a new bathroom suite, but because I was only a Mate I was not allowed to do any of the more interesting work. On quiet day's we would be left in the stores, and this was where I was most happy let me explain. The stores at McCarthy's Pliumbers was full of waste copper pipe left over from jobs that had finished, the problem was how to get the copper out of the stores without the storeman spotting you after trying to figure it out for some time I came up with the perfect solution, I had at this time a long top coat that I had bought in the second hand market in Cork, the pockets were torn so they went all the way down to the lining. I secured a hacksaw and went for the gun metal copper pipe ½ inch, or ¾ inch, and cut this into 6 inch lengths and then padded this

The Confirmation, the Suit and the Pawn

all around my lovely top coat, once out, I high tailed it to the nearest scrap yard. Oh it was a great feeling, I believe I got about 7½ shillings which was more that half my weekly wage. Unfortunately I was not in the stores very often, but anytime I was it was a bonus time. I suppose looking back now it was dishonest, but at the time I didn't think so, as far as I was concerned, the Firm had been paid for the job and these pieces of waste pipe were just waste.

The Suit

During our time in Churchfied I made my confirmation, this was a big day, it was the first time I would have a suit. Mrs O'Calaghan had an account with a company called Ray Murray, where she bought goods by the week. She took me to Ray Murray, where I picked out a wonderful suit I was really pleased with. In the meantime my father also bought me a suit a horrible tweed job, needless to say the Ray Murray suit went back and I was stuck with the tweed suit.

The confirmation came and went and one evening coming home from school I met my brother, with a parcel under his arm, it was my suit, my father had ordered him to go to the house and get the suit, it was his way to get some money, it was going to the pawn. This was not unusual at this time, many people would go to the pawn on a Monday, pawn the husband's suit to pay the rent. It would then be redeemed on Friday. The husband could then wear it to mass on Sunday, and the whole exercise would start again. I forget what happened to my first suit, but I lost no sleep over it. Later on in life I have owned very few suits.

CHAPTER FOUR

To Whom it may Concern

Get in, Get up, get out, get in, get up, get out, who the fuck was the nut case talking to his shovel in the next hole to me, let me explain, In 1969 I'm finished with the Sea, for the moment, so I decided to head for London, very little money, but in those days there was plenty of work in England. I headed for the Irish Centre in Camden Town, and got temporary accommodation there. While I signed on the dole and looked for a job, without having formal education there was not a lot open to me so Builders Labourer was about my pinnacle. The Company were based in Hampstead, and the job was at a place called Greenford, at Lyons tea Factory. It was some sort of extension, I had to lie about my age and say I was eighteen I must have looked eighteen as nobody ever questioned me about it. I had never worked as a Labourer before so I was trying to see what the other men were doing and follow their lead. The first morning the foreman, who luckily for me was Irish and originally from Waterford. The task was to dig the foundations for the extension, they were to be 3ft square by 6ft deep so we started with the pick and shovel, this other man left his post, and came back with a bucket of water, I thought has was going to drink it, but no, he put his shovel into it and in so doing was able to lift the earth with much more ease, instead the earth that I managed to lift just clung to the shovel. At the end of day one, he had dug the straightest nicest hole you would ever wish to see; I was not even a quarter ways down mine, next day he dug another one, as he did the day after, on day four, mine was finished, believe me it was a very poor excuse, just when the foreman told me "that's O.K." I hopped out and half of it collapsed again, and all the poor man said was that's O.K. Tom, just leave it. I think I will let you drive the Dumper instead.

Greenford was about one hour on the tube from Camden Town, so what I used to do was buy a half price ticket, if I was stopped I would say I hopped on at the Last Station, I'm sure you could not get away with that scam nowadays. I had made friends with a chap from Derry, who was also staying at the Irish Centre; it's so long ago now that I can not remember his name. One day he told me that some friends of his had a house somewhere in Kings Cross, one of the rooms had become vacant and would I be interested in sharing with him, of course I said yes. As it turned out there were twelve men all from Derry, except for two which were from Drogheda, this was the late sixties, and the troubles had not begun as yet, however all those lads could not find work in Northern Ireland they told me it was because of their religion, and where they came from. Most of them were working at Houston Railway Station as porters. We used to hand up the rent to one chap named Bugam Doherty, and being so young, I didn't know that he was very fond of the bookies, all was going well until one weekend he called us all together he told us that we were a few months behind on the rent, which was not forthcoming, so we had to get out fast. Someone had a van so we were able to put our bits and pieces in and for a few weeks, we lived in the back of the van. It was rough, but being so young, I felt it was like an adventure and quite enjoyed it. In the interim I had lost my job at Greenford, how that came about was, it was so far away, and such a long spin on the tube that I was mostly late for work in the mornings. It finally came to a head when, one morning I met the foreman in the Tube Station at 10 o'clock, he was going to the shop for the 10 o'clock lunch. Ah Tom just the man. I have something to say to you, I have something to say to you as well says I, O.K. go ahead says he, I'm leaving I said, you're sacked he said, and we both laughed.

Going to Manchester

One of the lads from Drogheda said he was going to Manchester and he asked me would I go with him of course I said yes and off we went on the train to Manchester.

When we got off the train at Piccadilly Station we put our cases in the left luggage and went to the employment office at the station, where we filled in the application form and we were given the start almost straight away, now we had to find some accommodation, which was going to pose us some problems, one night we had no money, so we slept in a toilet, other nights we walked the streets all night. However my friend knew someone in Manchester, evidentially he contacted him and persuaded him to give us a sub for a flat, until we got some wages from our new jobs. We got a flat in an area known as Salford, many years later I found out that Salford was known as a rough area, however I must say that I found the people very friendly, much more so than in London.

What I remember distinctly about my job as a porter in Manchester's Exchange Station was that there were two or three different shifts, on the late shift on Saturday nights, all of the Sunday papers had to be loaded into carriages to be taken all over the North of England. It was hard work but I'm sure we got extra money for doing it, and a special perk was that you had your pick of the Sunday Papers free. I also remember seeing the last of the Steam Engines, before they were gone out of service, they were awesome looking, yet looked so graceful, the brass parts gleaming, the paint work looking fresh, and steam bursting from the funnel, ah yes that's a sight we will never see again, mores the pity. One Sunday afternoon, I was working on one of the platforms, the task entailed that when the train came in was to make sure all the doors were opened, if anybody needed assistance with their luggage we were there to help, well this particular Gentleman, he was dressed in black, like a priest with a soft hat and a long beard. I later found out he was a Rabbi, he asked me to assist him and his wife with their luggage, one of the cases slipped away from my grip, as I was lifting it from the train to the platform, it rubbed against the platform and left a slight mark on the already well worn and half battered case. I thought no more of this incident until a few weeks later, the Inspector called me to one side. First of all he told me that a Rabbi had put a claim in, not just for one case, but for a whole new set.

Well I was somewhat taken aback, the Inspector asked me if I could recall the incident, and would I put in a report on the matter? At this stage I had already tendered my resignation at Exchange Station and my career as a Railway Porter was coming to an end, so I had nothing to lose, however the dishonesty of this so called Holy Man again amazed me. I filled out my report and, when I gave my report back to the Inspector, on reading it he said, well he will not get his set of cases now that's for sure. I left Manchester, said goodbye to my friend from Drogheda, whom I never heard from, or saw again, but was at least happy in the knowledge that the Rabbi had not got his cases. So I headed back to Cork and on to the next stage of my life, I wondered what was in store for me, would it get better, easier? I was after all I believed finding my feet, making my way, looking back now, hindsight is a marvellous thing, and what they say about Ignorance is Bliss is certainly true. Getting Better? No Chance.

LOVE'S MILLS,
This job was lifting 1 cwt. bags from a conveyer belt onto a pallet, 20 bags per pallet = I ton from 8 am in the morning to 6, and sometimes 9 pm, each day. I was shifting about 20 ton per day, that's 100 ton per week. Time spent at this job, about four weeks. The manager was surprised and told me that I had a job for life, my answer to him was, "Yeah, and that'll be about another week if I continue in this job".

Verdict: Even a horse could not do this job.

E.S.B.
The job; painting pylons. The height of these pylons was about 80 to 100ft. You had to climb up the frame, no scaffolding, they sway in the wind and you would need a head for heights. Wages £5.00 per day.

Verdict: Not one for the fainthearted.

POST & TELEGRAPH
Job; labourer, digging trenches for cables for the post office. This was the time that people began to think about getting a telephone installed. Hard, shitty work.

The summer holidays from school were not a holiday for us, we had to make sure that we got a job, messenger boy, helper on a lorry, anything at all.

My first summer job was as a messenger boy at M. J. Barry in Patrick Street, Cork. This shop was a woman's clothes shop of high quality with a large female staff, there was a brand new bike and Mr. Barry was a very nice man. A good job as messenger boys went, this shop long since has closed down.

Verdict: A good job for the time.

PADDY DONOVAN, BLACKPOOL
Manufacturer of Mattresses

Verdict: Terrible place. No sleeping on this job.

THE KITCHEN OF THE SAVOY CINEMA AND RESTAURANT.
Time spent in the horrible kitchen: 3 days

Verdict: Awful. But the food was wonderful

The Messenger Boy

THE MUNSTER FURNITURE CO.

This factory was at the back of the Munster Furniture Co. off the North Main Street. There were two of us tending this huge machine, the hairs of the coconut came compressed, to this factory, from Africa. The coconut hair was teased out and put through one end of the machine and came out the other end, nice and soft, to be used as the padding for mattresses. The other boy tended to be sleeping, or lying down, every time the boss came by. At the end of the first week, he was sacked, so I did all of the job myself and got both wages. However, I didn't stay too long as the dust and heat in there was pretty bad.

Verdict: I was off coconuts for life.

REARDON'S RESTAURANT AND BAR AT ST. PATRICK'S QUAY.

My first job, my two brothers before me had done this job, also after school, on a Wednesday and Friday. I would go and collect the laundry. Table cloths, towels, etc., they had to be taken to the laundrette for washing. For this chore, I received 2 shillings and sixpence and a good meal, chips, fish, etc. I was 10 or 11 years of age.

Verdict: A good start to my working life, an easy job, the meal was a bonus. The staff and the owner were very friendly.

PLUNKETT FRUIT AND VEG. COMPANY.

Oliver Plunkett St., Cork

Another after school-time job. Messenger boy. Everyday after school, 4 pm to 6 pm and all day Saturday. Wages £1- 10 shillings per week.

This was a delivery boy job, humping sacks of potatoes, vegetables, etc., to private houses, sometimes up 3 or 4 flights of stairs.

Verdict: A hard, tough job. The bike was like a tank, but it was the first bike I ever had so I was happy about this. On the down side, I was out in all types of weather and in the winter time with the wind and the rain, it was tough enough, especially considering that when I went home, I had to do my homework, etc. A good early lesson in the big world.

My first day as a trainee taxidermist - a polar bear behind the door. It was a joke the staff used to play on new employees. He was dead… I think

MARINA POINT NET.

A construction job in Cork Harbour, it was a very big plant and employed a few thousand men. I got a job as a rigger, i.e. lifting various pieces of pipes, tanks, etc., into position with a crane. One man I worked with, Michael Walsh, a man that had been at sea all his life and I quote him, "I have sailed the seven seas, but this is the first time I have been in a fucking sea of mud…"

We finished the construction, the plant opened to a big fanfare, top politicians, etc., saying how good it would be, "The plant was to manufacture urea".

Within a short time, the smells from the plant upset a lot of people in the area, soon after that the Net. plant closed down.

CORK AIRPORT: This job was in the old Cork Airport and my job was baggage handler, loader. In the '70's, in Cork, this would have been classed as a good job at the time. I was employed on a temporary basis.

CELTIC COASTERS: A Shipping Company that transported petrol and diesel from Whitegate, near Cobh, to the storage tanks of the Oil Companys in Cork City. This job was on a Coaster up and down the River Lee, a highly paid job, but dangerous enough.

NOONAN TAXI & CAB COMPANY
I ended up at the mad house, see page 68

J.P. WARD. TAXIDERMISTRY,
Kentish Town, London.
Yes stuffing animals,
Well not quite.
This Company, at this time were able to mount elephants tusks, buffalo heads, make cocktail trays from the soles of the elephant's feet, and so on. In those days all of these animals could be shot by wealthy English gentlemen and their skins could be dressed, or as in the case of the elephants, killed for their tusks, ivory was very expensive then, as it is today. I know that there is still a huge black market in trading in these wonderful animals; lions, tigers, cheetahs, all were shot at will for their skins. My job was to pare down the elephant tusks, this was done with a special knife you would have to pare it down so that it was

Working at Shandon with Sam Wright

completely clean and all the blemishes and scars were taken out. They also made umbrella stands from the feet of the elephant.

Verdict: Thank God all of these animals are now protected.

PFIZER'S PHARMACEUTICAL CO. AT RINGASKIDDY.

This was the construction of the Pfizer's plant at Ringaskiddy, I believe in the early '70's. I worked for a company called Bailey Meters, they did all of the instrumentation in the boiler house, the job lasted about 12 months and the wages were very good. It was interesting enough.

McCARTHY'S PLUMBERS, PLUMBERS MATE,

Verdict: Not allowed to become a plumber, closed shop, what a pity.

PULVERTAFTS, OLIVER PLUNKETT STREET, CORK.

Position: Storeman.

This company had a shop on Oliver Plunkett Street selling steel and copper pipes, welding rods, and brass and copper fittings, they had their own foundry where they made all of the fittings this was before the advent of plastic fittings for the plumbing and related industries. All of the fittings had their own code for example, a half inch bend was a no. 6 and so on. While I worked in Pulvertafts I had an accident. I was working one evening, and somebody came to me and asked if I could polish a letter box on the polishing machine, the flap of the box got caught in the wheel of the polishing machine, it caught my jumper and dragged me into it, I was caught under my arm and required 30 stitches, I was lucky I didn't lose my arm. When I went back to work they refused to pay me my wages. I claimed compensation and was awarded £500 pounds, after this I lost my interest.

Verdict: Miserable Company.

SAM WRIGHT, ORGAN BUILDER, CORK.

Position: Assistant.

Sam was a Dublin man and had learned the trade and skills in Dublin.

The ship of gold
(picture courtesy Marine Transport)

We worked in most of the churches and chapels in Cork and County, as well as some in Kerry. Some of the work was just a tuning job, other jobs might involve a full refit, one such job was St. Ann's Shandon, where they changed from a wind organ to an electronic one. This was a big job and kept us going for six months. Sam was an intelligent man with a good sense of humour.

Verdict: I enjoyed my time with Sam but it was time to move on. That fish keeps coming into my life.

S.L.D. PUMPS, INNISCARRA, CO. CORK
Position: Truck Driver.
This was my first truck driving job. The pumps were used for pumping water etc. from construction sites. I was somewhat nervous on the first day. There was a long body on this truck and a crane on the back to lift and lower the pumps from the truck. The first day I had to go to Nenagh in Co. Tipperary with some pumps, I had never been to Nenagh and did not know how to get there. I was told to go through Limerick, the Mallow Road at that time had I believe 102 bends on it. It was a baptism of fire, I was given no training with the crane in those days, you were just told to get on with it. The job was not well paid, but it was good training and experience and a good way to hone my skills as a driver.

Verdict: Tough but fair. Now if you want some directions to get to Nenagh, just… It's a long way to Tipperary, it's a long way to go…

D.J. O'CONNOR FURNITURE MANUFACTURE BARNEY.
Position: Driver.

A small furniture manufacturer in Blarney, its premises was an old school house, and my job was driving a large bedford lorry, Donal also recovered old suites of furniture, this was in the days when people didn't have the money to buy a new suite of furniture so they would chose a new fabric and have the old suite recovered, my job was to collect the old suite and return it when it was recovered, sometimes when we were collecting the old suite you could hear the rattle of money that had long ago fallen down the back of the settee, maybe by some, drunken father, sometimes we would find 2/6 sometimes maybe only a few pence, or 6 pence, anyway it was an unexpected bonus. Verdict: Donal was a good man, his factory has long since gone, and he died at a young age.

GILLIAN RUBBER AND PLASTIC, FARRANLEE ROAD, CORK.
Position: Driver.

Lee Young was the owner of this company, he had taken over the business in Dublin and opened a Cork branch. His brother John Young ran the Cork operation at about this time in the early seventies, people were just getting carpets, lino was dead, and the best underlay was tredare, all of the carpet shops wanted this underlay so business for Gillian was very good, when I started work they had a small lorry but very soon they needed a bigger one. The work load got much bigger also, but the wages remained the same. About this time Dallas was on the television and I think John Young got lessons from J.R. or visa versa. A mean man, his father I believe was one of the boys of Kilmichael as they came from Dunmanway.

Verdict: Shit Job.

M V. Sarsfield

In the late 60's I got a job as a Seaman on Vessel M.V. Sarsfield which was owned by a Company in Cobh, called Marine Transport. One of the jobs we got at that time was loading gravel at Passage West, in Cork Harbour and delivering it to Whiddy Island. The work on the oil storage facility had just begun. There were men from all over Ireland on the Harbour project, I believe there were 3 shifts and the money was very good, I remember vividly coming into Bantry Bay just as dawn broke the clear blue water, you could see, for maybe 20ft, the rugged but beautiful coast line, the tranquillity and peace of the place the sheer size of the bay. All that changed as soon as the supertankers started to use the facility. I'm sure the wild life and fish if they could talk they would tell you a good story about how their environment changed dramatically as indeed could the fishermen of the local. It took a terrible accident with a huge loss of life to finally close the operation.

Anyway back in the 60's all I was interested in was trying to make some money. We got an extra old halfpenny for topping up the gravel which in layman's terms means levelling the top, so we could close the hatches or hold covers as was the case in this instance. I would say we made that trip at least 12 times maybe more. One particular trip stands out in my memory. We left Bantry Bay on a Friday night, the Captain wanted to get home for the weekend, there was quite a swell and we took a battering. I think it took us about 36 hours to get to Cork. Now for those of you that don't know Bantry, is about 70 miles from Cork. I remember thinking at the time if I had crawled on my hands and knees I would have got there sooner. I remember the First Mate at the time a man called Creedon, an old timer, was in charge on the bridge when I went on watch to take the wheel, the ship as I said was taking a battering and was rolling about quite a bit, he started talking about some operation he had had on one of his eyes, he went into explicit details on how they put a needle into his pupil etc, I think his intention was to upset me, but I must report he failed, now if it had been the cook he would have had much greater success, because at the first sight if any resemblance of a rough sea, the cook would take to his bunk give you the keys to the store room so you would have to cook your own supper or whatever. However this was not so bad because you could really treat yourself to whatever you fancied. You know what they say, it's an ill wind that doesn't do someone some good.

That Summer was spent going to places like Barry Dock in Wales, Cardiff, Scotland, Holland, France generally all around Europe learning a little more as I went along but nothing was to prepare me for what lay ahead.

When I signed off the M.V. Sarsfield I think I was a little wiser. Romance wise nothing much was happening except one brief encounter in Cobh, I was walking this girl home and in an instance all of the street lights went out, I thought it was some sort of power cut but no I was informed that the Street lights were switched off each night at midnight. Anyway back to the girl, I must confess at this stage I cannot remember her name as I said nothing much was happening.

Back in Cork I don't remember much of the next 6 months or so, around September or October time I got a job on a ship called the M.V.Suavity it was owned by a Company by the name of Everards. They had quite a lot of these ships. Jim Murphy and another Corkman by the name of John Riley joined us as assistant cook the rest of the crew were English. We left Cork at the weekend in what was to turn out to be one of the saddest times of my life.

The voyage itself started out uneventful enough, I do remember going to take the wheel at Cobh and the seaman that was coming off watch gave me the course, S. by S.W. or something to that effect. I looked at him in disbelief as it transpired the compass was an old type standard compass I had never seen one before except in an almanack. However the Seaman explained it to me and I picked it up quickly after that. We were going to the Channel Islands and then discharging in the Thames estuary at a place called Gravesend. As I said the Voyage itself was uneventful and I must say the rest of the Crew were quite friendly and helpful.

When we got to Guernsey in the Channel Islands it seemed like a very nice place, there being no tax or very little, everything was a lot cheaper, Cigarettes, Beer, and Jewellery. I'm sure I must have went through everything I had what with the cheap beer etc.

When we left the Channel Islands we were heading for the Thames estuary. We anchored in the Thames at a place called Gravesend at about 2:30am. on a Friday night, Saturday morning, one of the Crew a man called Lawlor who had become friendly with myself and the other Cork man invited us to his cabin for a drink, as he was leaving the ship the following day. A very pleasant man of 28 years, well built and very good company, maybe after an hour or so the discussion turned to politics a very dangerous subject at the best of times add some drink, throw in an Irishman and an Englishman and you have a cocktail that in this instance would turn out to be lethal. I decided in my wisdom at this point to take my leave of them while things were still well in hand so I bade them goodnight and then went to my bunk. When I awoke in the morning maybe at 9:30 or 10:00 I went to the galley to have a cup of coffee when Murphy also appeared in the galley in a very drunken state and started to push me about, I told him in no uncertain terms to Fuck Off, go to his bunk and sleep it off. I remember, on the range at this time there was a big kettle of boiling water and he made some attempt to scald me with it. I remember saying to him that I would be happy to fight him when he sobered up and at this stage I knew that he was just out for trouble. I decided to go towards the Captains Quarters to see if I could get some help, I was halfway's towards the midship when I heard some shouting, on turning round I saw Lawlor smashing Murphy's head against the bulkhead, again and again before I had time to move, Lawlor caught Murphy and with one heave tossed him over the side of the ship and into the cold fast running Thames, I'm not sure how long I stood there but I remember thinking at the time serves him right, of course it didn't, nobody deserves to die like that for nothing in particular, but I suppose when your young and frightened it doesn't matter how, as long as what is frightening you is disposed of, in this instance it was poor 37 year old Murphy. God Rest His Soul.

I started to run towards where Lawlor had thrown him in, I looked over the side and could just about make out his head in the water, grabbing the nearest lifebuoy I threw it to where I had seen his face, but alas he was no longer there, the current was very strong and he being a non swimmer, was washed away in seconds. I can't remember how long I stared at that water.

Summing up of the number of jobs I have had, I must say that while some of the positions were interesting by and large they were boring and mundane. However, the experiences were valuable to some extent but it brought home to me what the lack of education means. I was unlucky enough not to be privy to the education system that pertained in Ireland at that time. Second and third level education was by and large only available to the middle and upper classes. In conclusion I have always felt cheated by the powers that controlled Ireland in those days, especially that I was most interested in education, and learning, so my university was the University of Hard Knocks and I got first class honours. How Bad.

CHAPTER FIVE

Nostalgia

During my time growing up in Cork, especially in the sixties, and seventies there were many characters'. FAX FAX the bells of Moscow, this was one of my earliest memories, this man would just repeat this sentence over and over again. I believe that he was suffering from shell shock from the war maybe the first, he was or looked old enough, I heard about Clondyke a character who got a ladies toilet built on Lavitt's Quay.

There was Josia who lived in Gurranabraher on the Northside of the city. The no.2 bus used to stop outside his house to let him out and a lady used to come out to help him in the door. Andy GA used to give a penny to children but his hand shook and most of the children were frightened of him. Johnny Rose used to stand outside Cashes Shop on Patrick Street, and whistle at all the women that passed by, he always had a rose in his lapel. I'm sure he brought a smile to most of the women that passed by.

There was holy Joe, the Rancher, fast Eddie, Tongy, Mattie Gum Boil, and I'm sure that there was many more that I didn't know about, alas most if not all of these characters are long since gone. I often wondered why these characters were not recorded in a book.

In Patrick Street we had the Savoy Cinema, the number one in Cork before television. This was the outing that most of the people of Cork aspired to especially on a Sunday night. This was the highlight of the week and those that had the money used to purchase their

*Crowds gather outside the Savoy cinema, Cork, for the start of
the Cork Film Festival, 21st May 1956*

(picture courtesy Irish Examiner)

Snowball fight at Fitzgerald Park, Cork, 1963
(picture courtesy Irish Examiner)

tickets a few months in advance irrespective of what film was showing. My memories of the Savoy was that when I eventually got the money to go there during the matinee, there was a Mr. Fred Bridgeman, he was the organist, he came up from the bowels of the earth playing this wonderful organ. It was fully lit up and the sound filled the whole of the cinema. The words of the songs he played came up on the screen and everyone sang along. It was wonderful. It was worth the admission alone to listen to Mr Bridgeman. It's a memory that has remained with me all down through the years, when he was finished he would disappear again down into the bowels to loud applause.

I also remember the Assembly Room's on the South Mall, better known as the Assems. The Assems was the cheapest of all the cinemas in the city but a very beautiful building. The facade can still be seen today. If my memory serves me right, there was a marble floor right through the foyer, with large framed photo's of film stars, such as Gary Grant, Doris Day, Humphrey Bogart etc. It was mostly cowboy films that I remember, and when one of the cowboys or Indians was shot a shout would go up, 'remove the body George.' George being the usher, would rush around flashing his flashlight, if he caught anyone they would be removed from the cinema. This was a great source of entertainment even more so if the film was boring.

Another cinema at that time was the Lido in Blackpool, on the North side. This was most definitely the cheapest, four old pence on a Saturday afternoon, Batman and Robin, Superman, the Cisco Kid. It was all there, there was a joke at the time, that went you could go into the Lido crippled and a miracle would take place, you would come out walking, walking, yea, walking with fleas.

Other cinemas at that time were the Pavilion in Patrick Street, the Capitol on the Grand Parade, the Ritz on Washington St, the Palace & the Coliseum on McCurtain St. Most, if not all of these cinemas have long since gone, more's the pity.

The other form of entertainment were the dance halls. My own recollection was of St. Frances Hall in Sheares St. and the showbands with the names of the Fontana, The Dukes, played songs there on Sunday nights. If you got a dance you would think yourself very lucky. This would have been the first time that many boys got the chance to engage with girls and visa versa.

Lots of Cork people have lots of good memories of beautiful Youghal Bay
(picture courtesy Irish Examiner)

Spring tides brought flooding to the centre of Cork. As children, it was such an adventure

(picture courtesy Irish Examiner)

She Loves You, Yeah, Yeah, Yeah

The Beatles, the Rolling Stones, the Kinks, Scott McKensie, they were all now making their names. *She loves you yea, yea, yea, Paint it black, 19th Nervous breakdown, Waterloo, Sunset, Let's go to San Francisco,* Long hair, hipsters pants, winkle picker shoes, rock and roll, teddy boys, mods and rockers, radio Luxemburg, the top twenty, motor bikes, scooters, mini skirts, the hoola hoop, desert boots. It was hip to be cool, it was cool to be hip.

I remember the Rolling Stones came to Cork and played at the Savoy, alas I was outside, I did not have the money to get inside. This would have been sometime in the sixties. The Arcadia ballroom was also very popular with the teenagers of Cork. Jim Reeves, the Who, were just two that I remember, I'm sure that there was many more down through the years.

On the Irish scene you had the show bands. They toured the country playing most of the hits of the groups from England and the USA from Kerry to Donegal, they travelled the length and breadth of the country. The Dixies, the Royal, The Miami, Adam Faith, The Troggs, Cliff Richard. We're all going on a summer holiday, a big hit for Cliff, it reminded me of my first and only holiday.

The Vincent De Paul were the organization that gave me my holiday. During that time many people were in receipt of charity from the Vincent De Paul. My recollection is that they used to call on a given night of the week, and they would give some money or vouchers to buy some basics like bread, porridge, and maybe a voucher for a bag of coal etc. These were ordinary people doing a wonderful service for the poor people of the country. Well, during the summer these same people gave up their free time and organized all the holidays for the children, from the organization of transport, to cooking, swimming lessons, and sing songs around the camp fires, these were very dedicated people. Over many years whenever the St. Vincent De Paul had a street or church gate collection. I always gave whatever I could. I gladly paid for my holiday many times over, and was delighted with my holiday, unfortunately it came to an end, too soon. Ringabella, the name of the place of my first and only childhood holiday.

A cowboy for a little while, a memory that would last a lifetime
(picture courtesy Irish Examiner)

Your Christmas tree here, or perhaps some holly, this was the place to buy.
No artificial trees here
(picture courtesy Irish Examiner)

Married too Young

I was married at nineteen years of age, much too young, with no experience of life as such. My wife's family were against the union, so at nineteen years we went to England and were married in London. The honeymoon was in Brighton, it was the height of the summer, and I got sunstroke and spent a number of weeks in bed. In hindsight this was probably a sign. My wife was homesick and did not settle, so after six months we were back in Cork. I remember the ship coming up the river Lee in Cork and was sick in my stomach just thinking of having to live again in Cork. It had been my wish and dream to go to Australia, where I know that my future would have been much brighter than now, back living in Cork. The first of four children arrived soon after, even his name caused a problem. We wanted to christen him Keith, but the local priest objected to the name. He said it was a pagan name, my response was surely what mattered most was the way he was brought up, anyway after a time the priest relented reluctantly. This was Ireland in the early 1970's.

Its hard for me to write about my marriage, as it was to say the least difficult, with no trade, or education to speak of, my work consisted of mundane jobs and with a wife and children to support, education was not an option. There were plenty of arguments and I believe that but for the children the marriage would have finished much earlier. I was working so hard, that I forgot about myself. My ex wife was a good mother, but for me was not a good wife, and fought with me about almost everything. The marriage lasted twenty years and I look back now with regret, the only good to come out if it was my children and when the break up came, I felt somewhat left down the lack of support from them, maybe they were intimidated by their mother. However after a separation period of maybe ten years, where my ex-wife and myself were supposed to be friends, I looked for a divorce, because I had met and wanted to remarry, the friendship came to an abrupt end and all hell broke loose. She made it as difficult as possible for me. I must have went to the Court five if not more times and had to pay her as well, so much for friendship with ex wives. In a strange way maybe it was a good thing because I know her real character, however it took me twenty years and more, it makes me think if we every really know anyone. It says a lot, to think that I can only write a few pages on this vast period of my life, maybe I could write more but I just feel at this point I don't want to or am interested enough.

A number of years ago I enrolled in a course to become a life and business coach. On finishing this course I started another course as a practitioner in LNP.

I found both of these courses were most beneficial to me and have served me well. Pity is that I did not have these skills earlier on in my life as I believe my life would have taken a different direction.

The Innisfallen

No piece of history or nostalgia about Cork in the 40ies, 50ies or 60ies would be complete without a reference to the Innisfallen. That wonderful ship, that for the main part took the poor, unemployed, those without hope hopefully to a better life in England. On Monday, Wednesday, and Friday she set sail for Hollyhead in Wales and from there the lucky travellers were transported by train to Paddington the main railway station in London.

At about 2pm on the day of departure the emigrants would start to assemble on Penrose Quay in Cork. Those that had travelled a long distance from surrounding counties, maybe Kerry, West Cork, Limerick etc. would have been on the road from early morning, all of the sandwiches would have been eaten, but along the quayside there were restaurants, and Pubs to tend to their hunger and thirst, when the time for sailing came, a lot of the emigrants would be the worst for wear, the few drinks would have taken its effect, and a lot of crying and sadness would be prevalent.

Going to England at this time was no small deal. Travel was not as easy as it is today and the chances were that if you went you may never get back to Ireland again. Most of the young men that went did not have an education so all they could hope for was a low paying low skilled job such as a builders labourer with Murphy's Men or McAlpines. This was tough physical work that took its toll on the men, many did not have any relations in England and the only company available to them was in the Irish Pubs in England, So in

The Innisfallen
(picture courtesy Irish Examiner)

The marsh district of Cork City. A slum area full of tenement houses where families as large as sixteen or eighteen children were often reared in one or two rooms. It has long since been demolished

(picture courtesy Irish Examiner)

This ship brought the hopes and dreams of many an immigrant a step nearer
(picture courtesy Irish Examiner)

The hustle and bustle of Patrick Street. It must be Saturday.
(picture courtesy Irish Examiner)

View of St. Patrick's Bridge and St. Patrick's Street, Cork, 1956
(picture courtesy Irish Examiner)

many cases after finishing a hard day's work they would go straight to the Pub, rather than back to their lonely bedsit, hence a lot of them got sick from neglect, and died young.

Other jobs available to them were porters in hospitals, hotels, waiters, lorry helpers, railways workers. As for the women most of them went into service as trainee nurses, hospital helpers, or maids in large houses, as well as the hotel and catering industry and factories, you could say that any job that the British didn't want the Irish took it. One such hotel in London that employed lots of Irish, especially those from Cork was the Cumberland Hotel, at the top of Oxford Street. This was a great start for any young person, as you would be fed and have contact with other Irish people that could help you find your feet. To my knowledge the Cumberland is still in business. Many thousand, maybe hundreds of thousands, left Ireland during this period. England while not ideal for the emigrants provided a lifeline and a ray of hope that better days lay ahead. As for England, they got their motorways, new buildings, and the best nurses in the world. My own experience of the Innisfallan is of the police taking me off of it in the early 60ies. I was 13 years of age but was desperate to leave Cork.

Henry Ford in Cork

Henry Ford's grandfather, John, left famine stricken Ballinscarthy, near Clonakility, West Cork, with his family for America in 1847. John's family had been evicted from land in Somerset, England.

John bought a farm in Michigan from an old acquaintance from West Cork, Henry Mayburg. On the night of the 1901 Census an 18 year old Henry Mayburg was staying at one of his great-grandfathers farms near Dunnamway in West Cork. A Patrick Ahern, from Fair Lane off Shandon Street in Cork City, had an adjacent farm.

John's eldest son William Ford 1826-1905 married Mary Gitogot 1839-1876 in 1861. She had been an orphan and had been adopted by Patrick Ahern and his family. Henry was born in 1863.

In 1914 the then hugely successful Henry Ford chose to build a 56-room mansion on a 1,300 acre tract of land approximately two miles from his Dearborn birthplace. He named the estate Fair Lane after Patrick Ahern's birthplace.

71

The Fordson team of the 1920s. Free state league winners.

You can have any colour you like, providing it's black
(picture courtesy Henry Ford & Son)

The Ford plant and an overview of Cork City

Another cargo of the car parts for Ford
(picture courtesy Henry Ford & Son)

The lucky workers with a good job in Fords
(picture courtesy Henry Ford and Son)

Ford cars for sale. Prefects, Anglias, Consuls, Cortinas… have I forgotten any?
Like the jobs, all since long gone.
(picture courtesy Henry Ford and Son)

Sad days. Who would have believed that Fords would close?
(picture courtesy Irish Examiner)

Workers Leaving Henry Ford & Son for the last time, Friday 13th July, 1984
(picture courtesy Irish Examiner)

Henry Ford's pivotal association with the south of Ireland city and country Cork is striking for two reasons: Henry was a Irish American protestant who was drawn back to his Irish family roots in Cork and as the tractors were beginning to roll off the line at the plant "he had decided to build in Cork in 1917". The war of Independence against British rule in Ireland was getting underway. Reprisals against Protestants resulted in the halving of their population in county Cork within the subsequent five years.

The Cronin's, The Chickens and Henry Ford & Son

After we were released from the Industrial School, we went to live in Churchfield on the Northside of Cork City. Churchfield was a relatively new council estate, exclusively working class. We lived at number 7 Churchfield Gardens with Mrs O'Callaghan "Nora", her husband "Christy" and their daughter Eileen. Nora had become our legal guardian and, while we were grateful for our freedom, there were many problems related to living at that house. Not least the fact that we never had enough to eat.

Next door lived, by coincidence, another family called Cronin. The father's name was Tom. He had two sons, Sean and Tom Jnr, and eight girls. I must confess that I have forgotten most of their names. Mrs Cronin was a wonderful woman with a heart of gold. Tom Cronin, the father, worked in Fords in Cork all his working life and would have been classed as very lucky. The Cronins wanted for nothing, and Tom Cronin always had the newest Ford model. He was also a keen gardener.

One early summer's day in the early 1960s, it came as no surprise to us when the Cronins got some one day old chicks. They soon began to grow and lay their eggs. Mrs Cronin was generous with the eggs and we got our share. As the long, hot summer wore on the days grew shorter and autumn was upon us. One Sunday dinner time there was a knock on our kitchen door. It was one of the Cronin children with a huge plate covered by a tea towel. He explained that they had killed the first of the chickens but none of the family would eat it. All the chickens had names, this one was called George. All of the Cronin children were crying. But it is an ill wind they say, so we sat down to a wonderful roast chicken. That Sunday and for many more thereafter, the knock on the door became a most welcome and happily familiar part of our Sundays for a time. The chicken co-op was, I believe, a converted Ford's box and the chickens were brought from the wages from Fords, so in a roundabout way during our childhood, Henry Ford and Son looked after us through the kindness and generosity of Mrs Cronin. May she and her husband rest in peace.

In 1930 when the population of Cork was approximately 80,000, Ford employed 7,000 and until the assembly operations were closed in 1984 Henry Ford and Sons Ltd., was the star company in Cork City.

Yes I remember that time well enough. It was front-page news on all the newspapers for weeks. It was a very sad time in Cork as thousands of families were left without a breadwinner. The repercussions were felt for many a long day indeed. I would say for years after.

The Ford Boxes

The various parts for the cars that were assembled at the Cork Ford plant were shipped in huge timber boxes, well constructed and as large as a small bungalow. Many people were interested in these boxes and when they had paid for them maybe 10 or 20 pounds they would be transported to places such as Crosshaven, a seaside village near Cork, where with the minimum of work they would be transformed into summer homes.

Barry's Tea

Barry's tea is and was synonymous with Cork and I can remember that the tea arrived in Cork in tea chests, these tea chests were very handy if somebody was moving house, or for storage. The tea chests were lined with silver foil and normally behind the foil would be a large collection of loose tea, so anybody that was lucky enough to get some tea chests from Barry's would normally have free tea for a few weeks or even months. To my knowledge Barry's gave the tea chests for free as well as the tea, a good and nice gesture, by a company that is still as strong as ever.

Christmas shoppers in St. Patrick's Street in December 1964.
Two weeks to go and counting
(picture courtesy Irish Examiner)

The wonderful North side of Cork City. "Here's up em all said the boys of Fair Hill"
(picture courtesy Irish Examiner)

Cycling to Mallow

Sometime in June or July in 1964, on a sunny warm evening, two of my friends and I decided to cycle to Mallow which is a town north of Cork city about 20 miles away. One of my friends had two bikes, one a messenger boy's bike with a large basket at the front. This bike, or tank as they were known by, belonged to the job that he was lucky enough to have. So at 8:00pm we set off on our adventure telling nobody as we thought that we would be back in a few hours, at first our spirits were high. We were laughing and singing, enjoying the fresh air, and all of the sounds of the country side, birds signing, cows mooing, and I on my borrowed messenger boy's bike.

The hours passed, one hour, two hours, three hours. At last in the pitch darkness we could see the lights of Mallow. The journey had taken much longer than we imagined, we were now tired, hungry and somewhat lost. Never having been in Mallow before, we decided to knock at a door and ask where the police station was. We believed that the police would bring us back to Cork. We told The lady of the house of our plight and out of goodness she gave us some jam and bread, which we wolfed down and were very grateful for. She then directed us to the police station.

When we got to the police station we relayed our story to them, but they were not very sympathetic. The best they could do was show us the road back to Cork. We had no lights on our bikes, were hungry and now very tired as well. The Mallow road in those far off days was a twisty winding road with nothing to guide us but the line in the centre of it. The mood now was very down. No talking or jokes, twelve, one, two o'clock, would we ever get back to Cork? Thankfully there was little or no traffic, maybe one or two cars passed us.

When we got to within the city limits a police car came and met us. The parents had reported our disappearance when we did not come home as normal. When we got home, well at best I got a hiding from my father and was kept indoors for about a week. I was sick of messenger boy's bikes and Mallow. Now whenever I see the cyclists in the Tour de France, I remember my Tour de-Mallow all those years ago on the messenger boy's bike.

Taxi to the mad house

Let me explain. When I was nineteen, or twenty, I had a job as a taxi driver with a company called Noonan's. The way it worked was the driver would get one third payment and the owner would get two thirds. The weekends were usually the best time as more people were out and about.

On one evening about 9:00pm I received a call to go to a public house on the North Main Street in the city centre called Mary Ryan's. I picked up my fare and he informed me that he wanted to go to Our Lady's "the Mad house". I thought that maybe he was a male nurse, or a doctor. He was well spoken and was making intelligent conversation. When we arrived at the entrance of Our Lady's I told him the cost of the fare. He replied "I have something to tell you", what's that? said I. Well it's just that I have no money to pay you and he started to laugh. I asked him if he was a nurse or a doctor, to which he replied "Neither, I'm a patient", and again he started to laugh. All I could say to him was, I think I should be in there and you should be driving this, he promised that if I picked him up again, he would pay me on the double. Needless to say I never saw him again.

We All Went Down to Youghal

In Cork City in the fifties and sixties not many people owned their own cars, indeed very few people could afford to take a holiday, so come the summer time the only escape for most of the working class was a day trip to Youghal.

The planning that went into this wonderful experience was meticulous. First and foremost, most, if not all, of the planning was done by the mothers, usually all of the street, maybe ten to fifteen mothers would make it a joint effort. All of the children would have a special job to do for weeks before. They had to make sure there was enough money for the trip, of course there was never enough as money was so tight. Buckets and spades, bathing costumes, maybe a new pair of shoes, t-shirts had to be bought. Finally the big day would dawn, the children would hardly have slept at all. The mothers would have been busy long into the night working final preparations, making sure everything was packed and, of course, last but not least, making the sandwiches; cheese, ham, jam and butter, anything you could afford, and if you were lucky maybe some biscuits.

Everyone would have been praying for a fine day and after early mass the throngs of day trippers would set off on their merry way to Youghal.

"We all went down to Youghal
we let the baby fall
me mother came out
and gave me a clout and turned me into a bottle of stout…"

The Railway Station

When the holiday makers arrived at Kent station in Cork there was bedlam; children everywhere, some babies in prams, toddlers, five, six and seven year olds, right up to twelve year olds. The trains ran every hour and every train was packed to capacity. Most mothers paid for themselves and maybe one or two children, however while the ticket inspector was being kept busy by the mothers, most of the children would dart through the gate and have boarded the train before the inspector would realise what was happening. I would say that most of the children travelled for free, the excitement was palpable and a loud cheer would go up when the train pulled away from the platform. As the train passed through the station on the way to Youghal, the excited children would continue to ask how much longer? Is it far from here? At long last Youghal came into sight, many for the first time could see the sand dunes and get their first glimpse of the ocean. When the train finally came to a halt the excitement had to be seen to be believed, children everywhere, mothers shouting, "Johnny, Johnny, mind your sister. Don't drop those sandwiches, what are you doing over there? Get over here at once!" Bedlam everywhere.

The donkey and pony rides, six pence a ride, could you afford it? If you spent your money now there would be nothing left for the Merries (the fun fair) afterwards. What the hell, children and their money are easily parted and so, after maybe half an hour, all the hard earned pocket money was gone. But the thrill of climbing onto the back of a real horse was worth every last penny, for a few minutes you could be Billy the Kid, Wyatt Earp, Jessie James, all of your cowboy heroes. Even though the ride lasted just a few minutes, the memories of the experience could bring back a smile long after you had left your childhood behind. The trip to Youghal was worth it alone just for the horses.

Next, hunger began to set in, children were annoying their mothers for food. "OK, OK, go to that house over there with the billy can and ask for hot water, there's three pence to pay for it, now hurry up." With the tea added to the boiled water, the tea was made and the sandwiches were laid out. Hands appeared from everywhere and many a slap and clatter was dished out before the sandwiches. At last they could wait no longer and so the feast began and, like a swarm of locusts, every last sandwich was devoured in record time, sand and insects included. But these sandwiches tasted better than ever, what's that saying 'hunger is a sweet sauce".

Next on the agenda was the swimming, "Mam, mam, Mary has been stung by a jellyfish." "Jesus Christ, get her out of the water," the mother would have been shouting as she rushed towards the sea. False alarm, it was just a bit of seaweed brushing her leg and so the day went by, on alarm following another, the masses now began to drift towards the fun fair. With all of the children safety corralled inside, strict instructions would be given to the eldest child, and most of the mothers and the few fathers would slip inside the nearest pub.

A glass of porter, or two, or three, a sherry, and a pint for himself. For mothers this was the best part of the day, maybe a few songs, and then all of the children would be rounded up, and with any spare cash left fish and chips would be bought and eaten on the way back to the railway.

The train journey back to Cork was a mixed affair, the mothers would be telling stories of long ago, about their experiences of Youghal. Some of the men would have a sing song, and most of the children would be asleep through exhaustion. On arrival back at Kent station in Cork, the long trek to the various suburbs of the city started and, all too soon, the summer holiday was over. But, boy, what a day!

CHAPTER SIX

The Boss At Last

Sometime in the Seventies

I now decided that I should start my own business, but what and how, I had no experience, knowledge, money, nobody to give me advice etc. how could I loose?

I decided on the nursery business baby buggies, cots, car seats, baby walkers etc.

After many months of research, pricing etc. I contacted one company in Holland that seemed interested in doing business, so I travelled to Holland, and met with the owner, a Mr. Lougberg, the Company's name was Mursarts and they manufactured a range of Prams, pushchairs, and buggies. After some discussions we agreed that they would send them unassembled, we would assemble them ourselves in Cork. This way I could get a better Price, I went to the bank with a set of projections as to how the business would go over three years, and they gave me a loan of £5,000.00 I rented a unit in the Old Distilleries in Blackpool, and waited for the first container to arrive, there was a few hundred prams on the container and I didn't have any sold. Well what could they do to me, at the very worst they could take the prams, I put an advertisement in the Evening Echo, opened to the public and waited for the customers and waited, and waited. After three days I sold my first pram. After that I got in my car and went to all of the nursery shops in the country. I must say I didn't have much success in Cork, one owner said to me 'I can't eat my dinner twice'. Roches Stores had a big nursery dept. But try as I might I could not do business with them, their buyer was a man called Austin Halleran from Dublin.

However, through hard work, long hours and being a jack of all trades, business began to increase, slowly but surely. I began to buy products in England, France, Spain, Italy, as well as Holland, Germany, and Belgium. On my first trip to Holland, I had no business experience, and even my briefcase was an old school satchel. Lousberg told me afterwards he felt sorry for my case, anyway he gave me very good prices and a great chance to make money. The early years were very difficult. The VAT rate at that time was 35% and the bank interest rate was as high as 28%

Business in Ireland in the 80's was very difficult. The way it worked was the goods would have to be paid for first, then when the goods got to the port the V.A.T. had to be paid, next you had to go and sell the goods, then wait for the shops to pay you, which in some cases could take up to six months, and always there would be something on the books, so in effect you had to act as the banker, as well as trying to pay back the bank, as well as your other overheads. However, I enjoyed working for myself, and over a number of years built up a very good business. I had accounts from West Cork to Donegal. At this time I was doing business with a Company in England called Albion Nursery goods, a Jewish man called Ben Wyman was the owner.

Ben had been doing business in Taiwan for a number of years, so in effect all he was doing was putting on his margin. I tried to get a closer working relationship with Ben, something like a joint company, alas, through many meetings we could not get an agreement so maybe it was time to go to Taiwan myself.

Taiwan

I had planned for about six months before I went to Taiwan, contacted various companies in Taiwan, got catalogues and prices, etc. not so easy back then as we didn't have the internet at this time, just a fax machine and postage. I first flew from Cork to Heathrow, then to Rotterdam, then to Hong Kong and finally Taipai, the Capital of Taiwan. I was flying for about thirteen hours, and as I remember I

Journey to Taipei, Mooncake Festival

spent a long time waiting in Hong Kong. I was met at Chang Shi Check Airport by a lady from the company, I was taken to a hotel called the Grand Hotel, this was a fantastic hotel up on a hill overlooking the city of Taipei. The first thing that struck me was the heat, while the sun was not shining, the heat hit me like, you know when you open the oven and the heat hits you, well just like that. When I waked into the hotel, the foyer was as big as a soccer pitch and the carpet was like, well if you fell down they would have to send out a search part for you, the pile was so deep. The Grand Hotel was built in the style of a historic Chinese House and many people from Taiwan came to visit it, because it was spectacular. The room was enormous, the bathroom was bigger than most double rooms in Irish hotels.

The trip consisted of being collected daily and visiting different factories, these factories were manufacturing nursery goods and supplied most of the markets in Europe. One night I decided to go out to the night market, most of the local people go to this market as the goods are cheaper. When it came time to go back to the hotel I decided to get a taxi, so I said to the taxi driver, Grand Hotel please. He looked at me with a blank expression, so again I said Grand Hotel please. He said something in Chinese, which meant that he couldn't speak English. So we drove around for a time he pointed out different hotels to me, then I had a brain wave, at the next Hotel I gestured that he stop and come with me to the hotel, when we got to the foyer I asked the receptionist if he spoke English, yes, oh thank God, I thought to myself.

Could you tell this taxi driver to take me to the Grand Hotel please. So after some conversation the driver understood and we were on our way back to the hotel. I can tell you that I never went anywhere after that without a hotel card.

On another day we were to go to the south of the country by car, on the way back there was a diversion because the motorway had been washed away it took us many hours to get back to Taipei. We stopped at a services which served rice. I was so hungry I learned to use chopsticks overnight.

Moon Cake Festival

The moon cake festival takes place every September. Legend has it that a common man fell in love with the daughter of the king, and she with him. The king decided that he was not good enough for her. So he banished him to the moon. Hence, the man on the moon, most of the people of Taiwan come to the Grand Hotel with their children to watch the fireworks display, and it's a sight to behold. Let me say after seeing this firework display I have never seen better, after all they did invent them.

The Barber Shop

One evening as we were leaving the office, the owner, his name was Bino, said he was going to the Barber shop and I should go with him. I said why not. So off we went in his car. We arrived at this plush entrance something like a four or five star hotel, red carpet etc. on entering the foyer we were greeted by a group of beautiful women forming two lines all bowing and smiling. This is not a usual barber's shop I thought to myself. After some discussion we were shown upstairs to a room, there was soft music playing, low lighting and two recliner chairs, which we were shown to, next two beautiful ladies entered and began to massage my head etc. as it turned out it was a massage parlour of high quality and the ladies were trained masseurs. Bino got a good laugh from it and I never forgot my visit to the barber shop.

The Christian

The driver in the Company was a young man who had only recently come out of the army, and on talking to him one day he said that he only had a Chinese name, and could I give him an English name. So going through a list of names he decided he liked Gary, after some discussion it was decided that he would be now called Gary. I thought at first that he was joking but from then on he was called Gary by everyone.

My trip and visit to Taiwan, proved very useful and was a wonderful experience. I learned about their culture, and their history, their wonderful manners, their respect for each other, their hard work,

The Grand Hotel, Taipei, 1989

and their word, nothing was too much trouble for them, and even though I was 'by their standards' a small customer, I was treated as their biggest, I got the opportunity to choose our own fabrics, wheels, metal etc for our range of buggies, I made sure that I picked the best. So when I came back the hard work started, I flew in a sample, and went to customers far and wide to secure orders for our new range. Our pricing was excellent and the colours seemed to please the specialist shops. A letter of credit had to be opened so the money had to be paid before the goods were shipped. It took about six months from the time of placing the order to receiving the goods, but when they eventually arrived it was well worth the trouble and wait. At last I had a range of products under our own brand. Lindy Ltd. It had taken so long, and many hours of hard work now the real work would start.

Over the next few years, the business began to become more successful, more accounts were opened and the name Lindy began to become known nationwide. Our relationship with the Taiwanese suppliers became more solid and trusting. The way that this business should work, is that you need one container in your warehouse, one on the High Seas, and one in production, and it takes some time to get to this stage, financially and to get all of the logistics right etc. We had got to this stage and we were looking around at some other lines. Not related to the nursery business, but could be sold to some of our accounts. Hall stands, nests of tables, mirrors etc. So after many years of struggling, things were beginning to come together at long last.

CHAPTER SEVEN

Screwed in Business
by a Corrupt Government

I was at a trade fair in Harrogate, in England, when I was approached by a retailer from somewhere north of Dublin. I did not know this man. He told me that I was being investigated, by who? I asked him, he would not say. I thought that it was the tax man, and the fact that I was fully compliant I did not give it any more thought.

A few months later, two men called to my office in Cork, they said that they were from the Director of Consumer Affairs and that they wanted to talk, they did not ring before, but came unannounced. McAnaing and another Mr Jerk, I can't remember his name, were the two corrupt Civil Servants. They told me that there had been a number of complaints about one of our products and they were having it tested in the U.K. and they would come back when they got the safety report.

Sure enough they came back within a short time, and said that they had got back the report and the buggy in question had failed the B.S. test. I was of course flabbergasted, they went on to tell me that one of the rivets had failed, I tried to explain to them that all of the rivets were the same, the rivets used on our products were the same as all of our competitors, it made no difference to them, however, they were not prepared to listen and laid down the law to me. Not to sell any more products, recall all of the products that were in the shops, show them everything I wanted to sell before I sold it etc. At this stage I asked them whose pocket they were in, and how much they were being paid. It was obvious to me that they were out to close my business down. Shortly after they went to the press and released a statement. I sent a similar buggy to S.G.S in London for the same test and it passed, I then sent the buggy with the test report to the Consumer Affairs office in Dublin, however they refused to accept it.

My business was now beginning to suffer, the shops that I had been dealing with began to lose confidence with us. Some shops were refusing to pay, however, we carried on and after the initial press release and the Director of Consumer Affairs best efforts to close down my business, slowly but surely I was beginning to get over the attempt by this corrupt organ of the Irish Government 'the Director's name was Fagan', but enter that other fabulous semi-state mouthpiece R.T.E.

One morning as I was going to work, I was ambushed outside my house by these jerks asking about my products etc. it seems that having failed to close me down they decided on a more stronger course of action, R.T.E. said that they were showing it on a programme called look Out. The presenters were Ainne Lawlor and Brian Dobson. I tried to get an injunction to stop the programme but to no avail. They tried far and wide to get some people to appear, but got only one woman. However, it worked perfectly for them. The next morning at 9.00 a.m. the phone started ringing and didn't stop for six months. The injunction cost me £1,000.00 pounds, I drove to Dublin, I employed a P.R. company, a waste of time. And what they set out to do they succeeded perfectly. They screwed my business.

I thought for a while that everything would work out, we had a democracy, I believed, and that the truth would come out. I contacted the Department of Industry and Commerce, the Minister was Mary O'Rourke. She was as useful as a hole in the head, the officers in the department were just as unhelpful, I contacted Michael Martin now Minister of Foreign Affairs again useless.

By now my business was in free fall the banks were looking for their money, and most of the shops I supplied refused to pay, and worst still I couldn't give away our products, never mind sell them. My life was falling apart. My marriage broke up at this time, the stress and pressure I was under was unbelievable and still there seemed no end in sight.

At this time in Ireland many people decided to leave, as jobs were at a premium. I had tried to start my own business and was successful. I paid my taxes, V.A.T. at the point of entry, and was employing a number of people. However, someone had got paid and I was causing someone trouble in their business. Corruption among politicians and civil servants was rife. They were all on the take.

At this stage I decided to change the name of the company to Trojan Ire Ltd. I had limited success. Next I went to Brussels and tried to see if something could be done. Again I ran up against a brick wall. I was running out of money and seemed to be fighting a losing battle.

I had exhausted all of the avenues open to me. I was tired both mentally and physical, my finances were in a bad condition, I had contacted the broadcast complaints commission, as well as Mr Bob Collins, Director General R.T.E. both fucking useless.

In the final analysis I could not carry on. My life's work, my marriage all destroyed by fascist right wing civil servants and inept, corrupt politicians.

I left and went to England and over the next four or five years I tried to build the business back up again. I was importing direct to England and every three or four weeks, I would come back to Ireland and continued to sell to my Irish customers, I look back now and can see that I had lost my drive and zeal, and try as I might I could not make a go of it, so in the end I had to give up.

In conclusion on this part of my life, these evil fuckers stole my life's work, ruined or tried to ruin my life and to this day I still don't understand and worst of all they were rewarded.

Now that I am writing this it is 2010, all of this happened over seventeen years ago, however, they still will not release the files that they hold on me, or the Company, under the Freedom of Information Act.

We are again entering a recession and no doubt they will be looking for entrepreneurs, bullshit, if you want some advice, take your talents to a country, where you will be respected and welcomed and your talents rewarded. Would I start a business in Ireland again?

No fucking chance.

CHAPTER EIGHT

Down But Not Out

In 1999 the then Taoiseach Bertie Ahern, apologised to the victims of child abuse in Ireland. He had no choice as his legal advisors had told him that if one of these victims went to the High Court they would win the case, so as a damage limitation exercise and a money saving scheme they started the miserable Redress Board, also the Commission into Childhood Abuse. The Redress Board and the appointment of the Commissioner, were all under the remit of the Dept. Of Education, the very, Department that were in charge when all of these crimes occurred. They also paid some groups of survivors who were compliant with the Department, and were happy to go along with the views of the Dept of Education, they were bought and paid for.

Having been locked up in two of these prisons, Greenmount in Cork and Upton in County Cork, I decided to get involved. I called a meeting in London and we formed a group to support and give information to each other. The stories I heard, the abuse, both emotional and physical shocked and saddened me. One was worse than another. It beggars belief that such abuses occurred in a so called Christian and Catholic country.

I felt that if they had at last faced up to the damage that had been done to innocent children, they would do the right thing, how wrong I was.

A Mr. Tom Boland from the Department was selected to oversee the operation and a very good job he did, so good in fact that he was promoted to a senior post in the Dept. Of Education. All he ever wanted to know was how many survivors were still alive, so he could do a number crunching job to see what the final bill would be.

The Government engaged with the religious orders who ran the prisons to see what they would pay, as it transpired they paid little enough, I recall about 127 million euros, and most of this in land that was not of much value. The Minister was a man by the name of Dr. Woods, so the religious orders who were paid by the government to run the prisons, starved, beat, and abused the children only paid a fraction and walked away with their wealth intact and no prosecutions of note.

The government decided on a method of payment, a scale, point system, so many points for different types of abuse etc. this favoured the government and meant the payments were less than if High Court awards were followed.

The lawyers, councillors, psychiatrists, etc. made money from the pain of the survivors on average the survivors were paid 60,000 euros and had to prove beyond doubt all of their allegations, they were treated like criminals in a horrible process.

One man I met during this time was Michael Collins.

Michael had lived most of his life in Cork, at various times he worked as a coal man, and a traffic warden. Michael grew up in Churchfied, a district of Cork. He was a little wild growing up, skipping from school etc. he was taken by the cruelty man and incarcerated in Upton, Co. Cork for seven years of his young life. He was abused both sexually and physically in the prison. The Order that ran this institution was called the Rosminian Order.

To say that his life was not easy would be an understatement, however, he got on with it as best he could, and I must say that he was always friendly to everyone he met, and would help them if and whenever he could. During the time of the Redress Board and when Michael's claim was being dealt with, he fell sick, first he collapsed and was taken to hospital for tests, where it was found that he had a tumour on his brain, within two weeks he was operated on, and then started to undergo chemotherapy, he was very sick at this time and his tumour was still active.

The Redress Board made him an offer of 80,000 euro, which he refused and decided to go before the Board in Dublin, even though they knew about his critical medical condition. I travelled to Dublin with Michael, and I thought that he would die on the way up.

They refused to hear his case unless I left the room, even though I was there as his support, I reluctantly left the room, and after a few hours they decided to reduce his award by 8,000 euro. He had no choice, but to accept their reduced offer as his health was getting worse, a very criminal exercise.

It was his wish to buy himself a new car, something he never had in his life, when he bought his car he was delighted, within a number of weeks he was advised by his doctor that he could no longer drive, he went downhill very fast after that, and died within a year.

It was a pleasure to have known and have him as a friend.

Most of the survivors that I know that got awards did not have any good luck with the money they received it was as if there was a curse on it.

As far as I was concerned myself I was awarded 43,000 euro, which I appealed and asked my lawyer if I could take my case to the High Court, he refused as I didn't have the money to fund such an action. I had to take their measly award. I had run up bills in operating the group, paying for the hire of a hall, flights, etc. all of which I paid for myself. As it turned out, even with my award, I was still in debt to the tune of 15,000 euro.

I was happy to do what I did, in trying to bring information and advise to survivors living in England.

In conclusion someone incarcerated for 15 years, getting an award of 60,000 euros is equal to getting fourteen euros per day. As I said a cynical exercise.

The commission set up by the government was the Lefoy Commission, however Justice Lefoy resigned due to the lack of co-operation by the Dept of Education. Next the Dept put in place Justice Ryan given him promotion from a District Court judge to a High Court Judge in the process, one of the first things they did was to drop the investigation into the Vaccine trails. These were trials carried out on children in institutions in the fifties and sixties, without permission, the trials were being carried out on cattle but it needed to be speeded up as polio was rife in Ireland, and they needed a vaccine like yesterday, so children in institutional care were easy targets. The church, government, Dept of Health, wellcome pharmaceutical Co, Dept of Education UCD were all involved in this nazi type of experiment. They came up with some legal excuses as to why they could not investigate any further. So there rests the vaccine trials. The Commission as I write, has completed its report. I hope it has a thick dust cover, as I believe unfortunately that's where its going to end up gathering dust on some shelf.

During my time that I was involved with the survivors, I met some wonderful people, most of them when they were released from the prisons, fled to England. They had little or not education and have lived their lives in a sort of twilight area, some of them had not even learned the basics of being able to read or write.

The Ryan Report into child abuse in Ireland has just finished and published its findings at a cost of 70 million Euros. The dogs in the street could have told you everything that the Ryan report published. Another sad day for Ireland as still they tinker with the problems that refuse to go away. Maybe some day somehow things will be put right.

CHAPTER NINE

Rockmount F.C. – Sport – F. R. Horgan's Boxing Club

From an early age, I was interested in sport and soccer was my favourite sport. I remember at an early age playing for a team called Southend United, the first game was at a pitch in Togher, in the Southside of Cork City. I scored 3 goals on my debut and the manager was very pleased with me, he encouraged me to make sure I was there for the next match.

However, I didn't have a pair of boots as the boots I had worn were borrowed, so I had to be happy with street football.

We used to have 'full internationals in Churchfield Gardens, on the green area, to us as children it seemed huge, now it is quite small. The Ryan's, Tom and Junior, the Monihan's, the McCarthy's, these were very enjoyable days, and if the result was not clear when we were called home, the game continued the next day. Many a good footballer learned his skills on the streets, indeed there was very little available, no training grounds, fitness centres, etc. yes the internationals at Churchfied Gardens were special.

I got very little chance to play football in my teens, I do remember on one occasion when I went to sea, we were at anchor in Casablanca and to starve off boredom a number of the crew decided to have a game of ball in one of the hatches, this was very enjoyable, it was difficult enough to play as the ship was inclined to pitch and roll in the swell off the harbour. As I said I didn't have much opportunity to play sports as I needed to work.

Fr. Horgan Boxing Cub

Fr. Horgan's boxing club was situated in a section of the Parochial Hall in Churchfield. The Parochial Hall was built a number of years earlier by the local men who gave their time and skills free and Fr. Horgan was overseeing the overall project.

One evening with nothing to do a number of us ventured into the boxing gym. Where we were welcomed, they gave us some skipping ropes and left us use the bags etc. on my second or third visit, they gave me a pair of boxing gloves, about 20 sizes too big, and put me in the ring with one of their young boxers. I believe that they were getting ready for a tournament, needless to say he was hitting me from all sides, and gave me a bloody nose, I liked the sport enough but was put into the ring too soon, I carried on for a period but lost my interest over time.

There were other times that I fought outside the ring, growing up in Churchfield was tough and you had to be able to look after yourself. I like to think that the training I got at Fr. Horgan's stood me in good stead.

Rockmount

One of my sons, Keith, played sport at school and soccer with St. Mary's a school boy soccer club on the northside, after some time he left and was asked to play for Rockmount, another Northside Club and rivals of St. Mary's. We progressed well and as a 16 year old played minor who would normally be a year older, a major trophy in Cork Minor Soccer. The Murphy Cup. We were pitted against Tramore, a Southside club, and hot favourites to lift the trophy. Keith scored the only goal of the match and Rockmount won the Murphy Cup as you can imagine we were elated.

The Rockmount Under 16 team was one of the best around they were unbeaten in all competitions, at local and national level. But with players like Roy Keane, Len Downey, the Martin Bros etc they were an exceptional team and won a lot of trophies.

During this time I had a van that belonged to the company. So most weekends I would drive the team to the matches, and collect £1 from each player as script for washing of gear. As for the van driving this was free of charge.

After a number of years I moved on from Rockmount. I was asked by U.C.C. to manage their junior team and as it transpired the intervariety competition was held in Belfast on that year.

The troubles in N. Ireland were in full flow at this time, and two incidents come to mind. The first involved a French student who was more interested in visiting the Fall's Road than playing soccer. So I asked him to ring his parents in France to obtain permission, which he got, and off he went to the Fall's Road.

The second item that came to mind, was during a match we were playing a N. Ireland College team who were beating us at the time. My son Keith was about to be sent off, and he called the ref. A N. Ireland Protestant Bastard, as soon as he got to the line, he said to me Jesus, I hope that they don't fucking bomb the hotel tonight. It gave me a good laugh.

A number of years later John Twomey from Rockmount called to me, and told me that the club was in bad trouble, had many debts- and owed the bank a lot of money. I was shocked and surprised as they seem to be going well, and had opened a bar at the grounds. After a number of meetings I agreed to get involved and became Chairman.

The first thing I did when I became Chairman, was to close the bar. If they were giving away the drink, and paying the customers to drink it they could not have been losing so much money. On the playing side, things were in dire straights. The teams were badly run, their kit was shabby. The whole structure was run down and the moral was at an all time low. Slowly, but surely with the committee, we began to turn things around. The bank debts were very big and it seemed that the bank could take the grounds from the club. So I negotiated a settlement figure and then we decided that we must sell one of the pitches. Planning permission was obtained for houses for three sites, the sites were sold for twenty five thousand each and the bank was paid in full. With the balance, the training areas were developed into a first class pitch, so at least the Club was again on a solid footing. So next I concentrated on the playing front. After some

The Rockmount Youth Team that won a Murphy Cup against all odds

Another good Rockmount Youth Team

*This is a U.C.C. University College Cork team that I managed. We got to the
cup final at Turner's Cross Stadium. As you can see, the ground was full...
well not quite. If you look hard enough you can see the one spectator and I had
to pay him to turn up. He gave me back my money and left at half time. We
lost 1-0 to Tramore Athletic.*

The name of the cup was the Carlsberg Cup... probably

initial mistakes, Terry Barrett was appointed player - manager of the Senior Team, I must say that he did a first class job, but after maybe two seasons, Terry felt that he was gone as far as he could go and stood down.

I then went after Billy Cronin 'no relation' an ex-player of Rockmount. After some persuasion he took the job and within one season had won the intermediate Cup, the top trophy for senior clubs in Ireland. I must say that a lot of the ground work was done by Terry Barrett. However, Billy is now in position for seven years and has taken the senior team from strength to strength, with many successes to his credit. A lot of the ex players are now involved in the management committee of the club, so all goes well for the club in the future. I always look for their results when I pick up the newspaper. A great deal of credit must go to these people who give up so much of their time voluntary but unfortunately it largely goes unnoticed.

CHAPTER TEN

The Shovel

During the builders labours days, I got a labouring job with a company called O'Shea Ltd. The site was near the employment office. In those days you had to bring your own shovel. The only problem I had was that I did not have a big one, if my memory serves me right the cost was 15 shillings. I asked amount but nobody had one, I started rummaging in the shed and low and behold I found what might pass as a shovel, let me explain, the shovel itself was tiny, not much bigger than the spade that a child might use at the seaside and the handle would be only suitable for a midget, nothing more to do but see if I could get away with it on the Monday morning the foreman put me doing some other work that I didn't have to use my shovel, so maybe around the third day I had to mix some cement. When he saw the shovel he looked at me in disbelief, I made some excuse, he told me that I must have a proper shovel or I would be sacked. The job lasted for a few months, but as least I had a shovel that I could bring to my next job. When I reflect now it brings a smile to me, the shovel that would have been too small for even a midget.

The Pigs

Jimmy Skally.
Jimmy Skally lived in Shandon Street, on the northside of Cork City.

Jimmy Skally, The Pigs and the Smell

The family owned a pub and Jimmy lived overhead, on a Saturday Jimmy collected waste food from the houses in the northside to feed pigs, that they reared or maybe he sold it to other pig dealers. So on Saturday mornings myself and a friend would go to Shandon Street and wait outside the pub for Jimmy to exit, we could be waiting for maybe an hour, maybe more. When he eventually came out, we would get in his van and head off to collect waste, our job was to go from house to house and collect a 5 gallon drum that would usually be around the back of the house. This would be full of waste food, we would take it to the van where Jimmy would toss it into a 20 gallon bin, and then we would return the empty 5 gallon bin. As you can imagine the smell was terrible, we would do this all day until all of the 20 gallon bins were full of waste, then he would take them to a pig place where they were unloaded. He would then go and wash the van, after that we would return to Shandon Street, where he would pay us. 2/6 each. I don't need to tell you that going home, we were hungry and smelly, but that day we had earned some money. Skally's pub is long since gone. Jimmy who knows, as for the pigs, well whoever ate them certainly got well fed pigs, and they must have tasted wonderful.

One Last Sweet Story

As a young boy of maybe eleven or twelve years, and living in Churchfield, I was fascinated with ships and the docks. However, there was one ship in particular that was of special interest to me; the chocolate boat. Yes, a ship full of chocolate.

This ship of gold used to sail from Cork to Garston outside Liverpool where there was a Cadbury's Factory. The chocolate crumb was a rough form of chocolate made in Co. Kerry, then taken by rail to the docks at Cork, and loaded for Liverpool. Such a huge amount of information for a boy, I hear you say. Well later in my life I was to have a closer relationship with the golden ship.

On one fine summer morning, I and a few of my friends had gathered like vultures near the carriages where the dockers were transferring the chocolate from the railway carriages to the ship. We were watching and waiting, maybe a bag would break and the chocolate would be fair game, as often happened. I'm sure the dockers had a hand in this. Break time came for the dockers and they left to have their smoke and tea.

This was our chance, we could not resist it. We moved closer to the carriage, one of my friends had a messenger boy bike with a big basket in the front. Yes he should have been doing his deliveries, but he was also too busy to worry about that now, at the door of the carriage was a huge bag of chocolate and, with a heave and a pull, the bag slid into the basket and we were running as fast as we could. "Jim, Jim they're robbing the fucking chocolate we could hear the angry shouts coming from the dockers behind us. "Come back you robbing bastards." It was all to no avail, the dockers didn't give much of a chase, their smoke and tea break was more important to them. The chocolate was so heavy that the back wheel of the bike was off the ground, so we had to lean down hard to keep it on the ground, but let me say it was well worth it. We gorged ourselves on chocolate crumb, destined for Liverpool, until we felt sick. The we started to trade it for comics and anything else we could think of that was of value to us. Yes, for once, we had struck gold.

Many years later when I was working on the M.V.Sarsfield, one of the voyages we made was, yes, you guessed it, we were consigned to take a cargo of chocolate from Cork to Liverpool and just like when, as a child, I was attracted to the boat, other children came and asked us for some chocolate. I remember giving a boy a small bag in exchange for a comic, 'The Dandy'. It bought a smile to my face then, as it does now.

Thank you Cadbury's. I've been a paying customer ever since, may I add.

I wonder if that ship of gold still sails?

CHAPTER ELEVEN

The Recent Past And The Present, Still Learning To Fly

As for me, my work now is Coach driving and tour guiding. I'm happy enough but grumpy, reflections on my life so far I would say that it has been tough, but what has kept me going is a sense of humour from the early days at St. Anthony's Road to Greenmount, Upton, Churchfield, Morocco, England. I can say it has not been boring. I have known and lost some good people through this time but let me say not so many. It has been my experience that if you can count the number of true friends on one hand and still have some fingers left over you are truly lucky. I have learnt to laugh at myself and the world. I am rich in many respects and in a strange way getting richer day by day. Yes, the University of hard knocks and life is by far the only university that matters.

A Leyland bus, long before power steering, some Raleigh bikes, ready for the off and a Ford Prefect, at the top of Patrick Street. In the background a sign for Pye Radios… now who remembers them?

(picture courtesy W.B. Kelly Publishers)

*Paper boys selling the Evening Echo or the Cork Examiner on Patrick Street, a
great way to make some money… 'Echooooooo, Evening Echoooooooo' they
used to sing at the top of their voices.*
(Picture courtesy of W.B. Kelly publishers)

A Triumph Herald and a Morris Minor. My first car was a Triumph Herald, I paid £20.00 for it. In the background the offices for British Rail, a very busy shop where tickets could be purchased for the boat and train to England

(Picture courtesy of W.B. Kelly publishers)

113

The gentleman standing looking towards the camera is, I believe, young Mr
Barry, at the entrance to Barry's shop, where I once worked as a messenger boy.
As for the dog, I hope he didn't think the man's leg was a lamp post.
(*Picture courtesy of W.B. Kelly publishers*)

Holy God, where have all the men gone?
(Picture courtesy of W.B. Kelly publishers)

Cork dockers, unloading a cargo of salt. No wonder our blood pressure is so high! Anyway, this was hard, thirsty work, so a few pints of Guinness in the evening was most welcome

(Picture courtesy of W.B. Kelly publishers)